The Girls' Book of Success

WINNING WISDOM, TALES OF
TRIUMPH, CELEBRITY ADVICE,
AND MORE

Edited by Catherine Dee

Megan Tingley Books
LITTLE, BROWN AND COMPANY
New York ∽ An AOL Time Warner Company

To Megan and Mary
Thanks for five fabulous opportunities

Compilation copyright © 2003 by Catherine Dee
Illustrations copyright © 2003 by Ali Douglass

First Edition

Library of Congress Cataloging-in-Publication Data

The girls' book of success : winning wisdom, tales of triumph, celebrity advice, and more /
    edited by Catherine Dee.
        p. cm.
    Summary: A collection of true stories, quotations, poems, and personal advice on
how to set and achieve goals, divided into such categories as "Success Stories,"
"Winning Wisdom," "Proud Poems," "Female Feats," and "Fabulous Facts."
    ISBN 0-316-73454-3
    1. Success—Quotations, maxims, etc.—Juvenile literature. 2. Conduct of life—
Quotations, maxims, etc.—Juvenile literature. [1. Success—Quotations, maxims, etc.
2. Conduct of life—Quotations, maxims, etc. 3. Women—Quotations. 4. Quotations.]
I. Dee, Catherine.

PN6084.S78G57 2003
646.7—dc21

                                                                                    2003046091

10 9 8 7 6 5 4 3 2 1

LAKE

Printed in the United States of America

Acknowledgments

The secret of this book's success? The accomplished girls and women who shared their tales of triumph and accounts of achievement. The response to my call for stories throughout girls' schools, including Miss Porter's School, Seattle Girls' School, Westover School, and Woodlands Academy of the Sacred Heart. The help of Emily Daly, A. T. Birmingham-Young and the Giraffe Project, Ida Huey, Nancy Gruver and *New Moon,* and Melissa Williams and Kathleen Smith of Runyon Saltzman and Einhorn, Inc., with the *Sacramento Bee* Woman's Day Professional Conference. The first-rate feedback from accomplished authors Elizabeth Carlassare and Julia DeVillers, star students Emma Lind and Katie Swisher, and my rockin' sister Sarah Dee. The support of the stellar team at Little, Brown: Megan Tingley, Mary Gruetzke, Shannon Langone, and Amy Geduldig. Ali Douglass for her awesome illustrations. John Javna, my role model. Alma maters Santa Catalina School and Pomona College. And all the usual suspects not so far named: Jonathan, Mom, Dad, Vicky, Ryan, Dick, Hal, Charley, Mike, Jeremy, Jessie, Jack, and Ben.

Thunderous applause!

Contents

Introduction

"The moment when first you wake up in the morning is the most wonderful. . . . Absolutely anything may happen," wrote nun Monica Baldwin. "The possibility is always there."

What magical things could *you* do with your morning, your day, your week, your school year, your life?

There are *so* many possibilities. You may decide you want to join a team or ace a class, run a large company or start a small enterprise, become a rocket scientist or a rock star, a senator or a saxophone player, a mayor or a mom, a firefighter or a foreign correspondent . . . or all of the above and then some! This is the twenty-first century — there have never been so many arenas in which girls can achieve. And, by the way, these arenas are not just what seems obvious: winning the first-place ribbon at the state fair, being student body president, getting an A on a math test. Success is living a full and rewarding life and accomplishing what's most important to *you*, so that when you're older and you look back on your life, you're satisfied and elated.

This book is about your dreams, but more than that, it's about how you're going to reach them.

Have you noticed that your dreams fill you with a kind of emotional spark? They make you feel revved up and alive. That alone is reason to smile when you wake up in the morning, but having the chance to transform a dream into a real experience is even more uplifting. It gives you a focus and a world to explore. The next thing you know, you're *there*, pinching yourself in proud amazement. Or maybe you're diverted along the way and end up in a totally different yet equally rewarding place.

The Girls' Book of Success will load up your mind with wise thoughts from women and girls who've reached goals that even *they* might never have thought possible. If you don't have clear goals, this book will help you explore possibilities. If you do have goals, it will inspire you to get moving, push ahead, and think *even bigger*. It will be a friendly mentor and handy reference on each of your many journeys to success.

How do I know it will do this? Because this is what it did for me while I was compiling it. This collection of wisdom is not a textbook — it's a treasure for your mind. Grouped together, the inspirational tidbits in this book practically generate electricity.

See for yourself! Read one or two pages and jump-start your motivation. Read the whole book and buzz with anticipation about what you want to do and how you're going to do it. Once you're rolling, go back and read a few quotes to keep on track.

Here's what's in the upcoming chapters:

Winning Wisdom

This section offers insight and advice from successful women: business executives, athletes, entertainers, government leaders, and activists, to name just a few. Their juicy morsels of achievement are just waiting to be put into practice.

Success Stories

This section brings you lengthier looks at success in the real world: the nitty-gritty on how girls and women set their sights and claimed their successes. Read these accounts of adventures ranging from trying out for a school performance to breaking a national sports record, from trying to get a job to becoming a famous CEO.

Proud Poems

Sometimes a poem is what best expresses the many emotions of success. This section looks at confidence, failure, and the nature of success.

Female Feats

Check out these quick bios of modern-day movers and shakers. These stellar women have rewritten history, shattered records, averted wars, broken barriers, transformed the business world, and influenced millions with their ideas, spirit, and drive.

FABULOUS FACTS

Which personality traits are associated with success? Whom do girls identify as their favorite role models . . . and whom do those revered women admire? This section reveals the fascinating answers to these and other success-related questions.

So now you know what's in the pages ahead: a ton of info to help you become a fabulous success. I think of *The Girls' Book of Success* as a "toolbox" that you can carry around with you, pulling out items as you need them.

If you find even one piece of advice in here that lifts your spirits or makes you ponder, I will be thrilled. If it helps you succeed, I will have succeeded. Why? Because this book is one of my dreams come true. When I was a teen, I imagined what fun it would be to write helpful books for girls. So I couldn't be more excited that you're holding this book in your hands right now.

Now it's your turn. How are *you* going to follow your heart, make your mark, and use your highest potential to live a wonderful life and perhaps even improve the world as we know it? Whatever your goal is, if you make it your intention, you can probably do it, or do something equally (or more) spectacular. As they say, "Shoot for the moon, and you'll end up in the stars."

Prepare for blastoff!

Catherine Dee

Far away there in the sunshine are my highest aspirations. I may not reach them, but I can look up and see their beauty, believe in them, and try to follow where they lead.

— Louisa May Alcott, writer, 1832–1888

Chapter 1

A Many-Splendored Thing

When most girls imagine what success looks like, they picture a pop singer performing for millions. A radiant actress on the red carpet at the Academy Awards. An Olympic gold medalist on the podium with a bouquet, tears of joy streaming down her face. A bestselling novelist with a stack of her books. A high-powered senator in the halls of Congress. Or the CEO of a large company, dressed in a suit with her arms crossed in a "don't mess with me" stance.

Each of these examples of success represents a huge accomplishment. But outstanding achievements are just the tip of the iceberg. What's in the rest of the ice? Unfamous things and less-obvious stuff. School sports team triumphs. A loving family. Third place. Overcoming relatively small challenges like quitting bad habits. Satisfaction with your life. These things are not as remarkable, but they're no less *successful*.

Success means so many things. What does *your* success look like — now and in the future?

Winning Wisdom

The measure of achievement is not winning awards. It's doing something that you appreciate, something you believe is worthwhile. I think of my strawberry soufflé. I did that at least twenty-eight times before I finally conquered it.

— JULIA CHILD, CHEF

I didn't have to become rich and famous to have a happy ending. I have enough food and a house. That's success.

— SHANIA TWAIN, SINGER

Success is more a function of consistent common sense than it is of genius.

— ANN WANG, BUSINESSWOMAN

Success is a very vivid emotion that sends shivers of delight up your spine and makes you feel like dancing and singing and shouting to let the entire world know what you have done.

— JESSICA LEVING, 13

It's not money; it's not titles. It's just wanting to go to work every morning and enjoying every minute of the day.

— SANDRA M. STASH, BUSINESSWOMAN

Successes, whether the small daily ones or the ones that get attention on a larger scale, are presents you give yourself. . . . Satisfactions that don't come very often, and don't stay very long.

— C. DIANNE SLOAN, COSMETICS CREATOR, BUSINESS OWNER

Success has nothing to do with how the world views you but [with] how you view yourself in line with your personal goals.

— JANET SKEES, COMPANY PRESIDENT, ENGINEER

There is no scientific answer for success. You can't define it. You've simply got to live it and do it.

— ANITA RODDICK, ENTREPRENEUR

Success Story
Everyday Victories

Six months ago, I would have thought that making cookies, finishing a game of miniature golf, or playing Foosball was nothing to brag about. Now, I know better. Success, like beauty, is in the eye of the beholder. What may seem like an everyday occurrence to some is a triumph to others.

I volunteer with adults and senior citizens who are developmentally disabled. Sometimes I look around and can't believe I get service hours at my school for doing this; I feel like I'm learning more from the people I work with than they're learning from me. Then a bowl clatters to the floor, a soda spills on the tile, I hear the plunk of pennies hitting the bottom of the toilet, and I wonder why I chose to spend part of my weekend up to my elbows in Elmer's glue. In these times of frustration, I think of how my friends are just chilling out while I'm cleaning up spills, setting up art projects, and putting away games. However, the irritating experiences are fleeting when I compare them to the happy moments.

I've learned more in these few weeks than I have from ten years in school. For me, success has gone from scoring a 100 on a test to scoring the first game of miniature golf a woman has ever played without assistance. A triumph is shooting free throws, not with my school's varsity basketball team but with a man who never had the opportunity to play in a real game. These are the accomplishments that keep the sun shining and the earth spinning. If they're not triumphs, then tell me: what are?

— EMMA LIND, 15

Proud Poem

Success

Follow your instincts and whether you dream
Of ballet, design, protecting a stream,
Biology, gardening, metalwork, law
Whatever you love . . . what puts you in awe.
Just be your best — no more, no less.
Your dream could come true; *that* would be success.

— JULEIGH HOWARD-HOBSON, WRITER

FABULOUS FACTS

According to a report by the Horatio Alger Association, the majority of teens define success as having close family relationships or friendships. Others define it as making a contribution to society, earning lots of money, living a spiritual life, becoming famous or respected, or being attractive to and popular with others.

According to a study of teens by G. Maassen and J. Landsheer, when several people pull off almost exactly the same achievement, each views it differently. Some of these achievers think of themselves as being pretty cool, while others feel they're just average or even as though they've failed. In other words, success is subjective.

Chapter 2

What Do You Think?

Ask anybody the secret of her success and you're almost guaranteed to get an answer like "I knew I could do it."

This won't come as a surprise, but studies associate an optimistic, can-do outlook with achievement. Do you believe in your ability, the possibilities, and your ability to take advantage of the possibilities? Because that's the first step. It's a good bet that your beliefs will move you toward certain actions and that those actions will propel you where you want to go.

Upbeat brain waves can take you very far indeed. So remember: think positive, keep an open mind, bounce back from bummers, and always look for the "silver lining," or for whatever you can learn from tough situations.

Look out, world; here you come!

Winning Wisdom

Belief . . . is the engine that makes perception operate.
— FLANNERY O'CONNOR, WRITER, 1925–1964

We are proof that whatever you put your mind to, you can achieve. This is just the start for us.
— BEYONCÉ KNOWLES, SINGER-SONGWRITER, OF DESTINY'S CHILD

As you soar to new heights in life, remember that the altitude you reach will be determined not by your aptitude, but rather by your attitude.
— BARBARA LANGFORD DAVIS, FINANCIAL ADVISOR

The way in which we think of ourselves has everything to do with how our world sees us and how we can see ourselves successfully acknowledged by that world.
— ARLENE RAVEN, ART HISTORIAN

No pessimist ever discovered the secret of the stars, or sailed to an uncharted land, or opened a new heaven to the human spirit.
— HELEN KELLER, WRITER, LECTURER, 1880–1968

Optimism is a choice. Cynicism isn't smarter, it's just safer.
— JEWEL, SINGER-SONGWRITER

Success Story
Now That's Something!

I have a Ph.D. in computer science. I have no idea how I got it, since I spent most of my time in school telling myself, *I can't do it!* I didn't just have a lump of doubt in the bottom of my stomach; you know, the kind that gnaws at you and says, *I really don't think I can, but maybe I can if I try harder.* No. It was a noisy, tearful, gut-wrenching I CAN'T DO IT!

I think I got a hint of what life is all about one evening when I was trying to do some particularly tough engineering physics homework. As usual, I was moaning and groaning. But then it hit me: I had a choice. I could do my best and turn in the homework, or I could give up and get a big fat zero.

I decided that *something* was better than nothing. With that, I got up the courage to do whatever I could and not worry about whether it was "good enough." That seemed to work, because I got an A– in that class. And while that grade didn't make me a rocket scientist, it signified that my *something* had made all the difference, in both what I achieved and what I learned.

Even today, I sometimes catch myself thinking *I can't*. But when I'm about to give up, I remember that something is better than nothing, and it could turn out to be an awfully big something.

— Dawn Myfanwy Cohen, information technology consultant

Female Feat

True leaders know that if their head and heart are in the right place, they can't *help* succeeding. Take, for example, Golda Meir (1898–1978), who helped found the state of Israel and was its prime minister (1969–1974). She was driven to find a diplomatic route to a peace settlement in the Middle East. When her efforts failed because the fourth Arab-Israeli war began, she stepped down but continued to serve in a key political role. "I was never affected by the question of the success of an undertaking," she said. "If I felt it was the right thing to do, I was for it regardless of the possible outcome."

Chapter 3

The Secret of Your Success

 Self-confidence and success go together like peanut butter and jelly. Before you can do much of anything, you have to feel genuinely good about yourself, and succeeding can't help but make you feel confident of your abilities.

Studies by organizations such as the American Association of University Women (AAUW) show that teen girls as a group are less self-confident than boys. Why? Factors include unrealistic media images of women (see chapter 17) and our culture's lower expectations for girls. When you lack self-confidence, you don't realize just *how* capable you really are, so you don't aim very high or accomplish very much.

When it comes to self-confidence, we're not talking about being stuck-up or assuming you're always right and everyone else is wrong. It's simply *knowing,* deep in your bones, that you're smart, capable, and filled with much more potential than you can even imagine.

Believe it because it's true.

Winning Wisdom

It is no secret that a strong, positive self-image is the best possible preparation for success in life.

— JOYCE BROTHERS, PSYCHOLOGIST

Confidence is at least half of everything you do.

— TARA HAMILTON, WAKEBOARDER

[Confidence] takes constant nurturing. It's not something [in which] you go in and turn on the light switch and say, "I'm confident."

— MIA HAMM, SOCCER PLAYER

Strut your stuff. Confidence is attractive.

— AMERICA FERRERA, ACTOR

Women have a tendency to "give up" instead of pushing themselves to stretch the limits of their minds and bodies. . . . If I'm going to be [successful], I must compete with myself to attain greater self-confidence.

— BARBARA BOWMAN, FARMER

The most significant contribution a woman can make to the success of all women is to increase her own confidence and sense of value. We are capable of anything once we believe we can do it.

— C. J. HAYDEN, BUSINESS COACH

Success Story
Extra! Extra! Read All About Me!

When I was ten, I decided my allowance just wasn't enough. I was too young to get a job, so I created a "newsletter" called *RNM* (*Rachel Needs Money*). On my mother's old typewriter, I wrote stories about my life and activities, and explained why I needed money. I even included random crossword puzzles and games. Then, at the end of the newsletter, I asked for donations. I sent this piece of work to family members and to my mom's friends.

I loved creating the newsletter and getting responses, and while I didn't get rich, it did tide me over until my next allowance. This project taught me to be proud of myself and that I could create a product with my own effort and talent. *RNM* was also a good way to learn about asking for money, something very important to know, especially for women, who are often hesitant to ask for raises or rightful compensation. And it was a lesson in being proactive about needing money rather than sitting around whining about it.

Now that I'm in my twenties, I sometimes get embarrassed when I think about how I "earned" money back then, but I do have to admit that it was a pretty cool idea. When you mix being broke with self-confidence, ingenuity, and a little creativity, anything is possible.

— RACHEL KRAMER BUSSEL, WRITER

Proud Poem

I know I am strong
   both in my convictions and in myself.
I know I am beautiful
   both inside and out.
I know I am powerful
   and growing more so.
I know I will do just fine.

— LAURA VEUVE, 15

Female Feat

Gloria Steinem founded *Ms.*, the first American magazine run by women, to promote feminism, which she called "the belief that women are full human beings." Throughout her career as an activist, she's faced countless stubborn barriers and continuing discrimination against women and girls but has still played a key role in improving the quality of life for the world's female population. During all of this outward-focused activism, what did she conclude? That self-esteem is *super* important if you want to succeed (her book *Revolution from Within* goes into detail). For all her achievements, she was inducted into the National Women's Hall of Fame in Seneca Falls, New York, in 1993.

FABULOUS FACTS

Can self-esteem ever be *too* high? Yes, if it's not based on anything of substance, says Dr. Jean Twenge of San Diego State University. She notes that while slogans like "I am capable" are popping up everywhere, they may actually cause inflated egos. *Accomplishr* are the key; once you do something worthwhile, you feel genuinely confident.

Want scientific proof that confidence and success are linked? According to a study at the University of Wisconsin, the lower your self-confidence, the faster you'll give up on your efforts to reach your goals.

Chapter 4

Making the Grade

 Your parents have probably drummed this message into your head, but it's worth repeating: *Study hard. Go to college.*

While there are accomplished people without college degrees, a college education is generally required for success. It opens doors and gives you the credibility you'll need to move ahead (especially when you look for a job later in life).

Once you've got that important piece of paper (in addition to all the interesting things you've learned), you'll be in great shape. Take your financial outlook, for instance. The U.S. Department of Labor tracks how much money college graduates and nongraduates (twenty-five years and older) earn. The average hourly pay for grads is around $20, but it's only about $12 for those without degrees. What's more, says *USA Today*, it's easier to get a job in a slow economy if you have a college degree.

Have degree, will succeed.

Winning Wisdom

Education is a precondition to survival in America today.
— MARIAN WRIGHT EDELMAN, CHILDREN'S ADVOCATE, WRITER

I would rather have my education and know who Dostoyevsky is than have a beach house in Malibu.
— JENNIFER BEALS, ACTOR

The biggest thing that my aunt shared with me is "Books before romance." So if you get your homework done first and you really focus on your school, romance will come later.
— LISA LESLIE, BASKETBALL PLAYER

The basic purpose of a liberal arts education is to liberate the human being to exercise his or her potential to the fullest.
— BARBARA WHITE, EDUCATOR

School is the first chapter in the book of your life.

— YUMIN LI, HIGH SCHOOL STUDENT

It's very important to have an education . . . to have something to fall back on, especially if you want to not only be successful but [also] be able to enjoy the fruits of your labor later.

— AALIYAH, SINGER-SONGWRITER, 1978–2001

School never ends. The classroom is everywhere. The exam comes at the end.

— ANNA QUINDLEN, WRITER

Success Story
Getting With the Program

I fell in love with computer programming the first time I compiled a program and it worked. That was in ninth grade. By the time I reached eleventh grade, I was taking college-prep courses, so I met with the guidance counselor to discuss my college plans. When I said I wanted a computer science degree, he dismissed the idea, saying it would be too hard for me. He gave me an application for the university I wanted to attend but didn't bother to mention financial aid or that I could test out of some of my college classes because my senior year of high school would cover much of the same information.

I told my mom I was signing up to pursue an education degree because the counselor said getting a computer degree would be too hard. She was incensed! She contacted the university, found me financial aid, and, even though she didn't know anything about computers or what my future might hold, supported my choice. Then, when I was accepted and some classes got tough, she listened to me and encouraged me to talk to the professors or consider my options.

College gave me the chance to explore my career choice, and my mom's determination taught me to not give up on what I wanted. If it hadn't been for my degree and my mom, I wouldn't be where I am today: working as a software engineer in a job I love. I've been at it for twenty years, and I'm still going strong.

— CAROL L. JOHNSON, SOFTWARE ENGINEER

Female Feat

Aspiring doctor Elizabeth Blackwell (1821–1910) applied to medical schools only to be turned away because she was a woman and because no one had ever heard of a female doctor. She finally broke through the admissions wall by applying to Geneva Medical School as E. Blackwell. The school eventually figured out she was a woman but let her stay as a joke. Her response was to go on to graduate and become America's first female physician (1849). In 1875, she cofounded a medical college for women.

FABULOUS FACTS

Do you like math? Don't fall for the idea that being a math whiz is a guy thing. Researchers from the University of North Carolina found that until age eleven, girls' math scores are actually *higher* than boys' scores. And then, by the end of high school, boys score only 1.5 percent higher than girls do.

According to *60 Minutes*, more girls than boys are getting college degrees. A Florida State University study found that while 66 percent of boys are shooting for college degrees, 75 percent of girls expect the same.

Chapter 5

What Makes You Tick?

This book is all about success. So, as singer Tina Turner says, "What's love got to do with it?"

Success is pretty much dependent on loving whatever you plan to do. If you're just into something for the status or, if it's a job, the high pay, or because someone keeps harping that you should be, success is not likely to come around, and if it does, you may lose interest.

Success needs a deep well of personal passion. When you're truly interested in something, you want to know all about it, and you have tons of energy to put toward it. Finding what you love might require some soul-searching, but you're bound to dig up one or more areas of interest.

When you commit to what you love in the name of success, the relationship is guaranteed to last.

Winning Wisdom

The things that one most wants to do are the things that are probably most worth doing.

— WINIFRED HOLTBY, EQUAL RIGHTS ACTIVIST, WRITER, 1898–1935

I come to work at six o'clock every morning. People . . . say, "Don't you have any hobbies?" I say, "What hobbies?" . . . This is where the excitement is.

— ROSALYN YALOW, NUCLEAR PHYSICIST

It amazes me that you would be able to play music for a living and be able to travel and see the world and get paid for it. Who thought of that? This isn't a job; it's so much fun.

— MICHELLE BRANCH, SINGER-SONGWRITER

To want in one's head to do a thing, for its own sake; to enjoy doing it; to concentrate all of one's energies upon it — that is not only the surest guarantee of its success. It is also being true to oneself.

— AMELIA EARHART, AVIATOR, 1898–1937

Receiving [an award] for something I love to do is like giving a bird an award for singing.

— Wilma Mankiller, activist, former principal chief of the Cherokee Nation

I couldn't go to work that I didn't like. I think I'd prefer to go . . . live in a tree.

— Penelope Cruz, actor

Success Story
The Path to Success

My professional journey began at age four when I declared to my parents and the world that I wanted to be a fireman. This was not some instinct toward civic duty. I simply loved the color red and thought the black-and-white dogs with spots were really cool. When I realized that being a firefighter was about more than the color red and the dogs, and that I couldn't paint like my artist mother, I assumed I would follow in my father's footsteps. He was a law professor and a judge, so I went to law school. I wanted him to be proud.

But it quickly became clear that I didn't like studying the law. And so this presented for me a gut-wrenching dilemma. Do I risk letting my father down or do I go do something else?

The decision tortured me, but I eventually made my choice. I left law school and went to business school. What seemed at the moment, especially to my father, like a random, ill-advised move was actually an important life lesson and a marker in my journey, which led me to an exciting career in business.

The lesson I learned is to love what you do or don't do it. Don't make a choice just because it pleases others or ranks high on someone else's scale of achievement, or even because it seems (perhaps even to you at the time) like the logical thing. Make the choice to do something because it engages your heart as well as your mind. Make the choice because it engages all of you. The freedom to choose is yours.

— CARLY FIORINA, CEO OF COMPUTER COMPANY HEWLETT-PACKARD

Female Feat

Marie Curie's (1867–1934) love of chemistry and desire to discover ways to heal people led her to the top of the physics profession. She was so captivated by the appearance of radium, which gave off a soft blue glow, that she kept some next to her bed. Unfortunately, she ended up dying from leukemia caused by the radiation, but not before winning two Nobel prizes: one in physics (1903), with her husband, and one in chemistry (1911) for discovering radium and polonium. In addition, she opened up opportunities for the scientists who went on to discover the neutron and artificial radioactivity.

FABULOUS FACT

How important is your personal inspiration in achieving your goals? According to a study by Bashaw and Grant, it's more critical than your intelligence, ability, and income.

Chapter 6

Dreams Do Come True

 Lie down, turn on your inner movie screen, and tune in to the Daydream Channel. In your perfect fantasy world, what are you doing?

Early in life, some girls have vivid images of who they want to become. For example, singer-songwriter Pink knew she wanted to sing "ever since [she] was three feet tall." Amelia Atwater-Rhodes, a sixteen-year-old published novelist, remembers making up a story about her stuffed animal when she was three, before she even knew how to construct paragraphs.

Don't worry if the images of your future aren't coming clearly into focus. The screen may stay blank until you take up a new hobby, enroll in a fun class, or get curious about something else that may serve as a starting point. Keep on watching; a new show will be starting soon.

Sweet daydreams . . .

Winning Wisdom

I stand for freedom of expression, doing what you believe in, and going after your dreams.

— MADONNA, SINGER

As you enter positions of trust and power, dream a little before you think.

— TONI MORRISON, WRITER

Dreams are . . . illustrations from the book your soul is writing about you.

— MARSHA NORMAN, PLAYWRIGHT

Figure out what you hope for. And the most you can do is live inside that hope. Not admire it from a distance but live right in it, under its roof.

— BARBARA KINGSOLVER, NOVELIST

You are your deepest driving desire. As your desire is, so is your will. As your will is, so is your deed. As your deed is, so is your destiny.

— LINDA C. DRAKE, CEO

You are the product of your own brainstorm.

— ROSEMARY KONNER STEINBAUM, EDUCATOR

It's good to have dreams and even better to follow them.

— ANN RODMAN, SOIL SCIENTIST

Success Stories
No Horsing Around

When I was seven, I dreamed of successfully riding a horse. I told my mom over and over that I wanted to ride. Finally, she gave in.

I thought riding would be easy and that I'd instantly be the best rider after only a couple of lessons. I soon discovered that the riders on TV, who make it look so easy, have worked really hard for years. I realized I would have to do the same thing if I wanted to be good. I reminded myself that riding was something I'd always wanted to do, and I kept at it. When my mom saw that I was so into it, she got me a pony.

At my first show, I didn't place in anything and was angry and disappointed with myself, but I was getting better. Then I started winning. It was the last show of the year, and out of sixty people, I won.

At that moment, I realized I had followed my dream all the way to what I'd envisioned when I was seven. Now I understand why believing in your dreams is the first step to making them real.

— CAROLINE GOTTWALD, 12

Betting On Success

I knew very early what I was supposed to do with my life, and I never let anyone tell me otherwise. When I was seven, I played in construction sites near my house and decided I wanted to be someone who built things. I stayed with that dream even though my high school didn't let girls take architectural drawing (mostly because no girl ever *had*). In college, I was told women didn't do well studying architecture, so I didn't enroll. But after college, I did general office work for an architect, and he taught me to draft.

When I landed my next job, I made a bet with my prospective employer that if after six months he could tell I didn't have an architectural degree, I would continue working for his low wages; otherwise he'd have to double my hourly pay. I won the bet.

What I didn't have was a good drafting hand, so I pursued the writing part of the architectural business. At age twenty-five, I became the first full-time female specification writer in the state of Washington and, later, the youngest and only female president of my professional society. Shortly after that, I opened my own consulting practice.

I don't know how many people can say they made their dream come true, but I count myself among them. The bet I made was a risk, but I can't imagine a better payoff.

— ANNE WHITACRE, SPECIFICATION WRITER

Female Feat

Did *Harry Potter* creator J. K. Rowling dream of becoming a legendary, record-breaking bestselling author with more money than the queen of England when she was a girl? Heck, no; her fantasy was simply to be able to walk into a bookstore and see a book she'd written propped on the shelf. "The most exciting moment for me . . . was when I found out Harry was going to be published," she explains. "Everything that has happened since has been extraordinary and wonderful, but the mere fact of being able to say I was a published author was the fulfillment of a dream I had had since I was a very small child."

FABULOUS FACTS

An on-line poll by Web site Monster.com found that most young people (65 percent) believe they can grow up to be anything they want to be.

What are girls' fondest hopes and dreams? According to a *Girls' Life* survey, 35 percent picture themselves famous. Another 26 percent of girls aspire to help others, while 20 percent dream of being a mom.

What kind of fame do girls envision? Preteen and teen girls in an informal on-line survey for this book were asked, "If you could do anything, what would it be?" Many cited careers, and these were the most popular:

- Actor
- Musician
- Director
- Writer
- Athlete

Chapter 7

Ready, Set, Goal

"I never thought about what I wanted to accomplish in life. I had too many things to do," said technology inventor Grace Murray Hopper (1906–1992). Apparently she wasn't much into setting goals. However, she's definitely the exception to the rule. You can bet that most successful people *do* set goals. They write overviews of what they want to do — mission statements — and "chunk" them into small tasks to complete.

Why are goals so key? Because people are easily distracted! Goals provide a critical focus that reminds you of where you want to go and keeps you pointed in the right direction.

So decide what you want to accomplish, and when: overcoming stage fright, learning to play the guitar, or winning a wrestling match, for instance. Write down each step you'd take leading up to the goal (including deadlines) by thinking *backward* from the achievement to where you are now.

Presto! You've got goals. Next step: act on them.

Winning Wisdom

Above all, I think it's important to remember what you are trying to accomplish and how you are going to do it.

— HILLARY RODHAM CLINTON, SENATOR

There is a world of opportunities out there for you, but it is ultimately up to you to establish your goals and set your sights as high as you wish, as high as the stars.

— SALLY RIDE, ASTRONAUT

Goals are dreams with deadlines.

— DIANA SCHARF-HUNT, WRITER

To attempt to climb — to achieve — without a firm objective in life is to attain nothing.

— MARY G. ROEBLING, BUSINESS EXECUTIVE

To tend unfailingly, unflinchingly, towards a goal is the secret of success.

— ANNA PAVLOVA, BALLERINA, 1881–1931

We must know who we are, so we can know what we want, so we don't end up wanting the wrong thing and get it and realize we don't want it, because by then it is too late.

— MARGARET CHO, COMEDIAN

The vital, successful people I have met all had one common characteristic. They had a plan.

— MARILYN VAN DERBUR, FORMER MISS AMERICA

I always wanted to be somebody, but I should have been more specific.

— LILY TOMLIN, ACTOR

Can we screw it up? Sure, we can screw it up. But, actually, not screwing it up isn't that tough. It requires sticking to your guns about where's the value and what [are] the goals.

— CARLY FIORINA, CEO

We write our own destiny. We become what we do.

— MADAME CHIANG KAI-SHEK, SOCIOLOGIST

Success Story
The Queen of Everything

When I was six, I told my father that my goal was to be a professional soccer player. In high school, the boys I had easily sped past in elementary and junior high soccer seemed to have doubled in size, and for the first time, trying out for the boys' soccer team made me nervous. But that didn't last long. By graduation, I had been voted Most Valuable Player for three years and had served as team captain for two. I also played football, and while kicking for the team, I was crowned homecoming queen. This accomplishment turned out to be my fifteen minutes of fame, and I appeared on television and radio talk shows and was featured in magazines such as *Sports Illustrated* and *People*.

After playing soccer in college, I accomplished my goal from girlhood: to play on a men's semiprofessional team.

There are no shortcuts to reaching goals, and I was willing to work hard to make them real. Looking back, I see that my greatest achievements turned out not to be the specific goals I had set, such as breaking records or winning awards, but more meaningul feats. One was overcoming barriers to women's participation in sports and knocking down all-male restrictions. I've always felt that a player should be defined by her ability to compete, not by her gender. I helped change a lot of people's perceptions. I finished my athletic career with no regrets. It's more painful to wonder, *What if?* than to lose; it's better to fear regret than to fear failure. I don't regret a single thing I did or failed to do, and I carry that sense of completion in my heart.

— TAMARA BROWDER HAGEAGE, PROFESSIONAL ATHLETE, COACH

Female Feat

When she was a girl, Kalpana Chawla (1961–2003) set a major goal that, at the time, probably seemed ridiculously impossible to many: to become India's first astronaut. But she was focused, driven, and motivated. According to one of her college professors, Atulya Sarin, she was never afraid of space flight and wanted to volunteer to go to Mars, even if she wouldn't be able to get back to Earth. She told *India Today*, "[Being an astronaut] is just something I wanted to do. It was very important for me to enjoy it." Her strategy when the going got tough was a rock-climbing tactic: "Focus on the next step, not on the ultimate goal." For her, every step was an important achievement. By the time she lost her life at age forty-one aboard the shuttle *Columbia* in 2003, she had triumphantly reached her goals and, in the process, helped the United States move closer to its space-exploration dreams.

FABULOUS FACTS

According to researcher E. Sigmund, successful people think about what they're doing and how they can improve their lives for at least fifteen minutes a day.

A report called "The State of Our Nation's Youth" reveals that teens have become more goal oriented as a result of September 11, 2001; many of them feel that they'll be expected to achieve more.

Chapter 8

Models for Success

You've probably heard that it's cool for girls to have a role model or a mentor.

What, exactly, is the difference between these two people? A *role model* is "someone worthy of imitation," such as a philanthropist, your congresswoman, or a CEO. A *mentor* is a caring, responsible person you trust, such as a teacher, a relative, a boss, or an older friend who believes in you, lends support, encourages you to consider various career options, and serves as a sounding board.

You can have several role models and mentors all at once. You can even have a mentor you've never met, simply by observing her or him from afar.

Whether you ask someone to be your mentor or she simply takes on the role without saying a word, make good use of this valuable guidance. Then you'll know what to do when someone can benefit from having *you* as her mentor.

Winning Wisdom

For every one of us that succeeds, it's because there's somebody there to show you the way out.

— OPRAH WINFREY, TALK-SHOW HOST

Mentors see things in you that you don't even see in yourself.

— CRISTINA MENDONSA, TV NEWS ANCHOR

The people you need to help make your dream come true are everywhere, and within your reach.

— MARCIA WIEDER, WRITER, SPEAKER

[Mentoring is] an amazing investment in another person. . . . And we who receive that attention in our lives should be very grateful, beyond gratitude.

— TWYLA THARP, CHOREOGRAPHER

It's important to have strong women as models for young girls. Moi is a strong yet fragile creature, a vulnerable but aggressive person.

— MISS PIGGY, MUPPET

Success Stories
The Success Files

When I was ten, I found my role model: Gillian Anderson, the star of *The X-Files*. She was everything I wanted to be and more. She ended up changing me in ways I never could have imagined. Thanks to her inspiration, I became interested in acting, which gave my life a new purpose.

For years, I longed to thank Gillian for bringing me out of my shell and helping me discover myself. The summer before I turned fifteen, I had a chance to attend a charity event she was hosting. It wasn't highly publicized, and it was pure luck that I found out about it. As one of two teenagers there, I was able to talk to Gillian, sit next to her, and take pictures with her. And the other teenager, Elice, became my best friend.

About a week later, Gillian invited Elice and me to the set of *The X-Files* in Los Angeles. When we arrived, she hugged us as if we were old friends. After we watched about five scenes and made several visits to her trailer, we walked off the set elated.

That trip showed both of us that dreams can actually come true. Since then, I've never dismissed a dream without truly working to achieve it. As I attend college and pursue an acting career, I'll call on that day whenever I need a little extra determination. And with that determination, I know I'll succeed.

— RACHEL LANE, 17

I'm a Poet, I Just Know It . . .

When I was sixteen, I decided to become a writer. Not just any writer but a poet. Not just any poet . . . a classical poet. But time and time again, my work was rejected as unfashionable, unmarketable. Some people told me not to give up. Others weren't as supportive. One harsh critic told me to "crawl back under the rock" I'd been under and take my "rhymes" with me.

I did not let this stop me. I decided to read my work aloud

wherever and whenever I could — at cafés, at colleges, and even at a theme restaurant.

One day, out of desperation, I decided to appeal to the British classical poet laureate, Sir John Betjeman (1906–1984). I reasoned that of everyone currently living and writing, he would offer me the critical look I needed. I sent a letter and some poems to him at Buckingham Palace. Did I expect an answer? In all honesty, no. But he answered! He told me to keep writing, that he liked my poems enough to tell me to keep writing no matter what happened. He said he had little doubt of my eventual success.

Although he passed away soon after, he changed the way I looked at my life. I realized I had been moving in the right direction all along — that I was right to continue, no matter what.

And so I have. I've since had my poetry published in magazines — all the while never straying from my classical style. I've won awards; I've seen my poems turned into songs and reviewed in fanzines. And whenever I get discouraged, I turn to the letter of advice (which I framed and hung on my wall) urging me to keep writing, from someone with little doubt of my eventual success.

— JULEIGH HOWARD-HOBSON, WRITER

Female Feat

In 1993, the Ms. Foundation for Women wanted to put girls in contact with real-life women role models at work and offer them new career ideas and inspiration. The result was a popular annual program, "Take Our Daughters to Work Day," which takes place at job sites across America on the fourth Thursday in April. In the event's first ten years, 71 million Americans participated. A poll by the Ms. Foundation and RoperASW found that the experience made girls more interested in education, had an effect on their decision to attend college (or a professional school), and made them think bigger about career goals and dreams. In 2003, the Ms. Foundation expanded its reach to include boys, renaming the event "Take Our Daughters and Sons to Work Day."

FABULOUS FACTS

Female role models (as opposed to male ones) are girls' best bets according to a study by Gilbert et al. Their research found that "female graduate students who identified female professors as role models viewed themselves as more career oriented, confident, and instrumental than did female students identifying male role models."

According to Girls Inc., an organization that works to empower girls, 99 percent of girls admire their mother more than anyone else because of her good advice.

Who are America's female role models' role models? Britney Spears falls into the mom-worshiper majority, proclaiming, "[My mother] taught me that I can do anything. That's what I live by. You know, I *can* do anything." Writer Alice Walker expands on that theme, acknowledging "our mothers and grandmothers, some of them moving to music not yet written." U.S. Supreme Court Justice Sandra Day O'Connor has a slightly broader view: "Our female predecessors . . . [who] had far more spunk and spirit than they were given credit for . . . I look up to them."

Another type of influential figure in your life might be an *idol*, generally defined as someone adored, often "blindly or excessively." In a study at the University of Calgary, 60 percent of the students said their idol had influenced their ways of thinking, and almost half said the person had inspired them to do something such as play a sport.

Chapter 9

Start Something

 Raise your hand if you've ever put off doing something that would help make you successful.

Are you raising your hand?

You're not the only one. Just about every girl, at some point, has had trouble getting started. You've heard of the law of inertia? A girl at rest on the couch tends to stay at rest on the couch.

As unmotivated as you may feel, get off the sofa and do *anything* to move in a productive direction. That could mean mapping out a goal, writing an outline, getting supplies ready, making phone calls, going to the library, going to practice after school, or whatever the first step is. You won't regret it.

Take one step forward, and inertia no longer has the upper hand. Then the law changes to "A girl in motion tends to stay in motion until she gets what she wants."

Winning Wisdom

The secret of getting ahead is getting started.

— Sally Berger, curator

I don't wait for moods. You accomplish nothing if you do that. Your mind must know it has got to get down to earth.

— Pearl S. Buck, writer, 1892–1973

I never lose an opportunity of urging a practical beginning, however small, for it is wonderful how often the mustard-seed germinates and roots itself.

— Florence Nightingale, nurse, reformer, 1820–1910

That little white ball won't move until you hit it.

— Mildred "Babe" Didrikson Zaharias, multisport athlete, 1911–1956

Nearly every glamorous, wealthy, successful career woman you might envy now started out as some kind of schlepp.

— HELEN GURLEY BROWN, EDITOR, WRITER

Look carefully before you leap. If you make a decision to do it, jump off the cliff running.

— SUZANNE LOCKLEAR, ENTREPRENEUR, BUSINESSWOMAN

Life is not a dress rehearsal. If you want to try something, just do it.

— PATRICIA SCHROEDER, FORMER CONGRESSWOMAN

I always believed that if you set out to be successful, then you already were.

— KATHERINE DUNHAM, CHOREOGRAPHER, DANCER

From now on, time will . . . go by like the wind. Whatever you want to do, do it now. For life is time, and time is all there is.

— GLORIA STEINEM, WOMEN'S RIGHTS ACTIVIST, WRITER

Success Story
Nerves Out Loud

They're always the same, the nerves. It should be enough that I feel good about my abilities, but it isn't. It should be enough that I won the award, but it isn't. This recital is just another opportunity to make a mistake. I imagine them all sneering and snickering. *How did she win? Just listen. She's completely unprepared.* It's a chance to prove myself to potential colleges, to the people who competed against me, and, most of all, to myself. If I fail, I'll have lost an irreplaceable opportunity.

The day has arrived. I'm striding toward the stage. My steps echo in the pit of my stomach. I sit and take a shallow breath, for that's all I can muster with my pounding heart. I place my hands over the keys.

As I play the first notes, I suddenly don't feel my fear; the nervousness subsides. A wave of relief flows over me. My hands are warm and vibrant, dancing over the keys. Each note rings when painted by my confident fingers. I'm thankful with every fiber of my being. I face an ovation instead of respectful, quiet applause.

I take my bow, vowing that from now on, I will end all perform-
ances this way, with this feeling.

— Katie Swisher, 15

Female Feat

A group of teen girls in Aniak, Alaska, has discovered that doing
something seemingly small — in this case, becoming volunteer
firefighters in a tiny town — can herald new dreams and influ-
ences. One of the girls in the all-young, all-female group of
"Dragon Slayers" is Erica Kameroff, who has responded to approximately one hundred emergencies. Although many of these
incidents were minor disasters, such as a spot gasoline fire, her
ability to help people has given way to a desire to be a doctor. "I
feel prepared for anything," she told *YM*.

FABULOUS FACT

According to a study at the University of Nebraska, people regret
not taking action much more than they regret having failed at
what they attempted.

Chapter 10

Just Say Yes

That's going to be tough. . . . It's very competitive.
You'll never be able to do that.
WHY *would you want to do* THAT?

Aargh. Why do people have to rain on your parade?

Some of them may honestly believe they're doing you a favor by being "realistic" so you won't be disappointed if you don't achieve your goal. Some are good at lecturing you but actually don't know what they're talking about. Others may feel insecure about what you're doing — maybe they're jealous or afraid *they'll* somehow lose if you win.

So don't take negative comments to heart. Examine them closely and use them constructively, if at all; think of each as a grain of salt. If you get a whole pile of salt, run the feedback by someone who's optimistically levelheaded. It's fine to take another look at your goal and make adjustments. Just remember that many a girl has succeeded after being told she never would and that you have every opportunity to join their ranks.

Winning Wisdom

When someone tells me there is only one way to do things, it always lights a fire under my butt.

— PICABO STREET, SKIER

People will always try to knock you in life — and knock your dreams. In a peculiar way, that's not such a bad thing. In the end, it gives you an opportunity to prove you want it enough and that you're strong enough to keep going.

— CHRISTIANE AMANPOUR, FOREIGN CORRESPONDENT

Don't let anybody tell you how hard it is, just do it.

— NIA VARDALOS, ACTOR, SCREENWRITER

You know when someone says you can't do something, and you feel like, *You know what? I think I will. I think I can, and it's going to be fun!*

— JUDY MCGRATH, PRESIDENT OF THE MTV GROUP

Of course it's important to be a good listener . . . but it also pays, sometimes, to be a little deaf.

— RUTH BADER GINSBURG, SUPREME COURT JUSTICE

Always accept your compliments. Ignore the others.

— MELANIE REAGAN, RADIO NEWS DIRECTOR

[Naysayers] are irrelevant to us. There will always be people out there who doubt you and your abilities, so one just has to use them as motivation to prove them wrong.

— MARION JONES, SPRINTER

If I'm going to be criticized for doing what I believe in, I might as well just keep doing what I believe in.

HILLARY RODHAM CLINTON, SENATOR

Success Story
The Best Man for the Job

Vote for Julia; she's cool-ia!

OK, it's not the greatest campaign slogan in the world. But cut me some slack — I wrote it when I was nine, after my fourth-grade teacher announced that our class would elect a class president.

I stood in a huddle on the playground with my girlfriends. Yeah, I wanted to be president. I loved the idea of being a leader, of helping our class be its best.

The boys knew something was up. "One of you girls isn't thinking about running for class president, are you?" sneered Dave O. "Girls can't be president," his sidekick, Dave C, said laughing. "Don't even bother," Dave O continued. "The boys won't vote for a girl."

Looking back, I realize I should have laughed in their faces. But they planted a seed of doubt in my mind. There *were* more boys in the class. Maybe I shouldn't even try; if I lost, I'd feel worse. If I didn't try, at least I wouldn't lose.

Back in class, my teacher asked for nominations. My friends looked at me, but I shook my head.

"I nominate Dave O," said Dave C. Dave O piped up: "I'm going to have Dave C for my vice president."

Wait a minute. Now I realized why they were trying to talk me out of running. They wanted it for themselves.

If I didn't at least try, I would kick myself later.

"Anyone else?" my teacher asked. "Are Dave and Dave unopposed?"

I hissed to my friend, "Nominate me!"

"I nominate Julia," said my friend. Dave and Dave shot me dirty looks.

I ran for class president, and I won (yeah!). But wait, that's not the important part. I learned that people who may seem sincere aren't necessarily looking out for your best interests. I'm not saying to ignore people, because they often have good advice. But when someone tries to talk you out of something you really want to do, think about their motives. And then, don't let them.

— JULIA DEVILLERS, AUTHOR

Female Feat

In 2000, when the economy took a dive and the overinflated Internet sector "bubble" burst, some people predicted that the popular on-line flea market eBay would fail like most other Internet businesses did. Meg Whitman, president and CEO of eBay, proved those people all wrong, and then some. She not only kept eBay going but also turned it into an extremely profitable, wildly successful global company. And she's not finished yet.

Chapter 11

Go for It!

 During a tennis match, Venus Williams's doubles partner and sister, Serena, gave her a little lecture. She didn't think Venus was playing at full capacity. Did Venus sulk and throw her tennis racket? No. She sat and thought about Serena's wise observation. All of a sudden, a light went on in Venus's head, and she realized that there was no point in being simply mediocre. "When you commit yourself to something, you . . . have to go," she says. "And as long as you have to be there, why not give it your all?"

Why not, indeed? Aside from the fact that you often *must* give 100 percent if you want to succeed, doing your best is a smart habit.

Want to stand out, take a stand, be outstanding? Go for it!

Winning Wisdom

Most people live and die with their music unplayed. They never dare to try.
— MARY KAY ASH, ENTREPRENEUR, BUSINESS, EXECUTIVE, 1915–2001

The dedicated life is the life worth living. You must give with your whole heart.
— ANNIE DILLARD, NATURALIST, WRITER, POET

Sometimes I fall, but landing every jump isn't the point. It's the attempt. It's the effort.
— SARAH HUGHES, FIGURE SKATER

You are the artist of your life. It's up to you to decide whether your canvas is a stunning reflection of who you are — or an ordinary painting that would get hung up in some cheap hotel.
— CHERYL RICHARDSON, AUTHOR

I would rather sing one day as a lion than a hundred years as a sheep.
— CECILIA BARTOLI, SINGER

Never look back and say I wish I had.
— Jodi F. Solomon, company president

I love to see a young girl go out and grab the world by the lapels.
— Maya Angelou, poet, writer

People get specific information about what to do in their lives, and they don't pay attention, especially if it's impractical. Usually there's a window of time in which you can act on a dream like this, and if you don't, then the opportunity is gone.
— Judith Orloff, psychiatrist, intuitive

Don't avoid the game. Your work in the several decades when your schooling is over will be the most important part of your life. . . . Make it count.
— Patricia Wald, U.S. Court of Appeals judge

You are *supposed* to stretch everything that you are. . . . You are *supposed* to have a big life so that when all is said and done, you can say to yourself, with feeling, *I loved my life so much*.
— Mary Wells Lawrence, advertising executive

Embroider this on your psychedelic pillow in glitter thread . . .
"Life is a Movie Starring You."

— JENNIFUR BRANDT, WRITER

Success Story
Going for the Gold

I never thought of myself as an athlete, but one day, I decided to see how far I could run with my dad. I followed him three-quarters of a mile before I started huffing and puffing and had to walk. The next day, I did it again. Then I was hooked.

In August, when I was up to two miles every other day, I heard about a 5K race in October. I was crazy about the idea . . . until I started all the hard training. I dashed up hills, did sprints, and ran up to four miles, often feeling ready to collapse; but since Dad kept going, so did I. Dragging myself out the door was the most difficult part. But I got physically and mentally stronger.

When race day dawned, time seemed to both stand still and rush by. I hoped to finish in seventy-fifth place or better, and in thirty minutes.

When the gun went off, I wove through the runners and found

my pace. I felt strong and confident, and in what seemed like no time, I sprinted across the finish line, bursting with happiness and lack of oxygen.

When the results were posted, I glanced at the bottom of the page and slid my eyes up the list to find my name. My jaw dropped. I'd come in *first* in my age class and twenty-fifth overall.

I was an athlete! And while I received a shiny medal as proof, it was my smile that shone the most.

— MOLLY GRAMES, 15

Proud Poem

We never know how high we are
    Till we are asked to rise
And then if we are true to plan
    Our statures touch the skies —

The Heroism we recite
    Would be a normal thing
Did not ourselves the Cubits warp
    For fear to be a King —

— EMILY DICKINSON, POET, 1830–1886

Female Feat

In 1997, Madeleine Albright became the first female secretary of state, also making her the highest-ranking female government leader in U.S. history. What did she do on her watch? She brokered the Middle East peace talks, among other achievements. "Democracy may be conceived by dreamers," she said, "but it is made real by doers."

FABULOUS FACT

"Going for it" does not necessarily mean doing it *all* — being the career woman, raising kids, and doing housework. At a *Fortune* magazine "Most Powerful Women in Business Summit," 30 percent of the women in attendance had househusbands. And of the fifty women on the *Fortune* list of Most Powerful Women in 2002, more than a third had a full- or part-time stay-home husband. "Remember that saying, 'Behind every great man is a great woman'?" says *Fortune*. "Well, forget it. As corporate women continue their climb up the ladder, the reverse is increasingly true."

Chapter 12

Work It

When you see a basketball player dunk a basket on TV, it looks so easy. What you *don't* see is all the hours, days, months, years — sometimes entire lifetimes — of hard, gritty work.

Is it worth it? Ask basketball player Kylie O'Neill-Mullin, eleven, who used to be terrible at foul shots. "It was embarrassing when everyone was watching and I couldn't hit the rim," she says. So she established a routine and practiced it for months. Then, during the last few seconds of a tie game, she was fouled. Here was her big moment of truth! She took the shot, it went in . . . and her team won the game.

Succeeding at something almost always means tons of toil and dedication, but look at the rewards — a photo finish, attaining goddess status at your school, an unshakable feeling of utterly ecstatic joy. Is it worth it? You bet!

Winning Wisdom

It takes twenty years of hard work to become an overnight success.

— DIANA RANKIN, WRITER

You can have unbelievable intelligence, you can have connections, you can have opportunities fall out of the sky. But in the end, hard work is the true, enduring characteristic of successful people.

— MARSHA JOHNSON EVANS, NAVAL OFFICER

What separates a winner from the rest of the pack is not raw talent or physical ability; instead it is the drive and dedication to work hard every single day.

— LINDA MASTANDREA, WHEELCHAIR ATHLETE

People seldom see the halting and painful steps by which the most insignificant success is achieved.

— ANNIE SULLIVAN, 1866–1936, TEACHER TO HELEN KELLER

One only gets to the top rung of the ladder by steadily climbing up one at a time, and suddenly all sorts of powers, all sorts of abilities which you thought never belonged to you — suddenly become within your own possibility.

— MARGARET THATCHER, FORMER PRIME MINISTER OF ENGLAND

I thrive on hard work. . . . Even the words we use to express hard work — *effort, exertion, strain* — have a ring to them I find irresistible.

— MALI SASTRI, MUSICIAN

I work 24/7, and still it's not enough.

— VERA WANG, FASHION DESIGNER

For you to be successful, sacrifices must be made. It's better that they are made by others but failing that, you'll have to make them yourself.

— RITA MAE BROWN, WRITER, POET, ACTIVIST

I was taught that the way of progress is neither swift nor easy.
— MARIE CURIE, PHYSICIST, CHEMIST, 1867–1934

Work is part of my genetic code; work is in my blood. My response to adversity is always the same: work harder.
— JANET JACKSON, SINGER

Success Story
Flipping Out

Diving was the thing I was most afraid of. As a member of the diving team, I knew I would have to do a flip, but every time I got on that board, my stomach lurched. Every part of my body got nervous, especially my back. I would try over and over, and every time I would smack my back hard on the water. Then I would sit out and cry until I was ready to try again.

One day I woke up determined to do a flip. I went to practice, got on the board, jumped, and smacked. Every time, I tried harder, but every time, I failed. But I had to try again.

The next time I got on the board, I jumped so high and threw so hard that I landed in the water not on my back but on my *feet*. The sensation I got when I finally nailed this was overwhelming: I was in heaven.

Now I'm doing flips all the time with ease.

— MARIA CAIN, 11

Female Feat

Growing up in racially segregated Birmingham, Alabama, Condoleezza Rice took to heart her parents' belief that hard work opens doors; she knew that in order to succeed, she'd need to not only work twice as hard but also be *much* better than anyone else. She graduated from college when she was sixteen, got an advanced degree at twenty-six, and began a career as a professor and then a provost at Stanford University. The next thing America knew, she had moved into several key governmental positions, culminating with her role as the first female national security advisor. Where will her strong work ethic take her next?

FABULOUS FACTS

Simply putting effort toward a goal won't necessarily get you there. According to a study at State University of New York, you must supply *efficient* effort, not just spin your wheels.

Who studies the hardest? According to the American Enterprise Institute for Public Policy Research, in high schools, girls are apparently working harder and getting better grades than guys are.

Chapter 13

Hang In There

When she was young, business executive Gail Lione aspired to work for her congressman. However, most members of Congress were (and still are) so busy that they hardly had time to take a coffee break. So Gail sent the congressman a polite letter. When she got no response, she waited a week and sent another. And another and another, until he sat up and took notice, then called Gail and eventually hired her.

Is it any wonder that the one quality successful people have in common is perseverance? It's hard not to be impressed by someone who not only knows what she wants but is willing to ask for it (repeatedly if necessary) and work like a dog to get it. Stick-to-itiveness stands out starkly in a world where people don't always go after what they want or stay committed to getting it.

Keep on pushing. If that doesn't work, vary your strategy and try again. You never know when you'll suddenly break through.

Once you get what you're dreaming of, don't toss out your perseverance. Keep it handy, because you'll be needing it from there on out.

Winning Wisdom

It's not what you do once in a while, it's what you do day in and day out that makes the difference.

— JENNY CRAIG, BUSINESSWOMAN

Never give up . . . for that is just the place and time that the tide will turn.

— HARRIET BEECHER STOWE, WRITER, SOCIAL CRITIC, 1811–1896

I have much less talent than I have guts. But because I kept persevering, I took the little bit of talent that I have and made it the best it could be.

— SHARON STONE, ACTOR

You may have to fight a battle more than once to win it.

— MARGARET THATCHER, FORMER PRIME MINISTER OF ENGLAND

Life is like a ladder. You may take one step up and then two down, but you just have to keep going until you reach the top.

— NAHARA RODRIGUEZ, SWIMMER

Prevail, stay in the race. A quitter never wins, and a winner never quits.

— BRENDA J. CULPEPPER, RECORD-LABEL PRESIDENT

You have to keep going until you hear *yes*. If you have a great idea, stick to your guns.

— ASHLEY POWER, 16, WEB SITE CREATOR

Satisfaction comes from enduring the struggle, from doing more than you thought you could do, from rising — however briefly — above your everyday world, and from coming, momentarily, closer to the stars.

— SUE COBB, MOUNTAIN CLIMBER, AMBASSADOR

I long to accomplish a great and noble task, but it is my chief duty to accomplish humble tasks as though they were great and noble. The world is moved along, not only by the mighty shoves of its heroes, but also by the aggregate of the tiny pushes of each honest worker.

— HELEN KELLER, WRITER, LECTURER, 1880–1968

Success Stories
From Zero to Hero

Fitness testing consists of five events and has two possible rankings: national and presidential. Presidential is the best, but every year I would get boring, plain national.

The coaches explained the five events we had to accomplish for the presidential award. One was pull-ups. Eleven-year-old girls had to do three. Well, I could do zero.

I decided that in the two weeks I had to train, I would find a way to do them. Unfortunately, there was no shortcut — I would have to work hard every day.

I asked my coach if I could practice on the high bar. I stood on the block to reach it, grabbed the bar, and hung there. I pulled with all my might. Guess what? I did one! My dad helped me practice. A few days later, I trotted over to the pull-up bar in the gym and, without even realizing it, did two.

It was time for the testing. The other kids counted as I went up: "One . . . two, two and a half . . ." And then I fell. My face turned red with anger. Even though I could retest later, I almost gave up then and there.

I didn't practice for about five days. My mom said this was good because resting is just as important as practice.

When it was my turn to retest, I grabbed the bar and went for it. Everyone was counting, "One . . . two . . . come on, you can do it . . . THREE!"

That was one of the proudest moments of my life. Not because I did three pull-ups, but because with practice, motivation, and other people believing in me, I'd gone from zero to three. The coaches used me as an example in all the other gym classes. Wow!

— LARA SHUGOLL, 11

Fishing for a Compliment

"Work that line," O. D. whispered in his lilting Bahamian voice.

The sun burned hot and gold on my back as I squatted in the water. I did not move. I didn't even breathe; I was so afraid of disturbing the silence or breaking my concentration. The bonefish spooked too easily to take the risk.

I was new at this fishing game. It had taken me all morning just to be able to see the fish. Although I'd followed O. D.'s pointing finger, I couldn't see the schools he assured me were there. The fish were aluminum torpedoes in motion, blending perfectly into the shadowy ripples of the water. All day he had overlooked my clumsy casting. Over and over, I'd screamed in frustration as my line went flying in the wrong direction and ducked my head in embarrassment when, as my jig slapped the water, the fish bolted away.

But no matter now. I gently tugged the jig through the water. "Steady. Work it," he repeated as I closed my eyes and ground my teeth.

My fingers realized it as they felt the line go taut, but my mind didn't until O. D. cried, "You've got one!"

I laughed as I reeled in my fish. Gently lifting it out of the water, I put my lips to its fishy mouth. Then I put it back and watched as it swam away.

— MARENE EMANUEL, BUSINESS OWNER

Female Feat

Christiane Amanpour was told that her appearance, the length of her name, and her British accent would make it tough for her to realize her goal of becoming a foreign correspondent. When she started as a low-level staffer at a cable news network, her boss belittled her dream. "Sometimes tears of frustration would pour down my face, but I never let on and I was determined to press on," she recalls. "[The experience] taught me to have absolute clarity of vision . . . to have the courage and stamina to pursue my goals." Her perseverance paid off when she was able to move into a writing position; her big break came when the network needed a reporter in Germany. Today, she's on television screens around the world, her name is a household word, and her accent is part of her appeal.

FABULOUS FACT

A study at Florida State University found that girls who are persistent spend lots of time reflecting on what they've already accomplished and focusing on what their current project demands.

Chapter 14

Bumps in the Road

 Have you ever done an obstacle course? It's a lot like the path to success.

You can see some obstacles coming a mile away, but mostly they just seem to pop up out of nowhere when you smack into them. They could be as seemingly minor as people's misguided comments or as major as physical accidents and natural disasters.

The fascinating thing about roadblocks to success is that some have an uncanny way of *helping* you succeed. For one thing, they require you to think on your feet and to call on all your resources to get past them, reaffirming your commitment. Also, when you're feeling frustrated by an obstacle, you don't know the positive things it could be hiding. Looking back on your completed journey, you may see that what seemed at the time like a terrible mess simply redirected you to where you *really* wanted to go, or to even more rewarding success.

Winning Wisdom

There are always going to be bumps. Figuring out how to get over the bumps, that's what's really fun.

— ALICIA SILVERSTONE, ACTOR, PRODUCER

When something happens in our lives that forces us to reach deep into the storage room where we have these hidden strengths and resources, and we use them, we become incredibly confident because we know that if *this* didn't destroy me, what can?

— ISABEL ALLENDE, AUTHOR

The best possibility is to be lost and to be finding, to be moving forward.

— SARAH FERGUSON, DUCHESS OF YORK

Show me a person who has never made a mistake, and I'll show you somebody who has never achieved much.

— JOAN COLLINS, ACTOR

Successful people aren't the ones who happen to get dealt great cards. They're the people who get dealt the not-so-great cards but make them work beautifully.

— ATOOSA RUBENSTEIN, MAGAZINE EDITOR

Sometimes you have to fall down and skin your knees, and some dust has to come up around you, before you can be quiet and see the stars.

— BOBBIE KINKEAD, STORYTELLER

Too often when all is well, we slip into the false joy and satisfaction of the material and a complacent pride and faith in ourselves. Yet it is through struggle that we find redemption and self-knowledge.

— CONDOLEEZZA RICE, U.S. NATIONAL SECURITY ADVISOR

The things we overcome in life really become our strengths.

— ANN BANCROFT, ADVENTURER

Success Stories
Listening to the Heart

When my parents found out I was deaf, they figured they would simply handle it, that it was not a big deal. *No* was not in their vocabulary. They tried to raise me as any child should be raised — with love and respect. The only thing they did differently was put up a yellow caution sign on our front lawn that said "Deaf Child Crossing." It didn't bother me; in fact, it made me feel important.

I loved acting, and by the time I was twelve, I was peforming in a variety of musicals and shows. I wanted to be an actor so badly that I could taste it. During this time, I was performing at the Center on Deafness in Northbrook, Illinois. There, I had an opportunity to meet actor Henry Winkler (Fonzie on *Happy Days*), and I told him how much I wanted to be an actor. But someone took him aside and whispered that he shouldn't encourage me because as a deaf person, it would be much too hard for me to achieve my dreams in Hollywood. I was destined to fail, they told Henry.

Henry nodded politely. As it turned out, Henry himself had defied the odds to become a success — he was dyslexic. He turned around, knelt down, looked me right in the eye, and said, "Don't ever let anyone get in the way of your dreams. Follow your heart and your dreams will come true."

What a defining moment that was for me.

Nine years later, there I was on Henry Winkler and his wife Stacey's doorstep with an Academy Award in my hand. "What now?" I asked. Though I had been given Hollywood's highest honor, there were reports that my victory was only a pity vote and that I would never work in Hollywood again because I was deaf. I was devastated. Henry and Stacey took me in, and just like when I was twelve years old, they helped me refocus my energies and set my sights on achieving my dreams.

It's been sixteen years since that day on the doorstep, and I haven't stopped working. I'm an actress, an author, a producer, an activist, and the mother of three wonderful children. And I'm still dreaming and still following my heart.

Deafness cuts you off from people only if you let it. Remember, the real handicap of deafness does not lie in the ear; it lies in the mind.

— MARLEE MATLIN, ACTOR

A Downhill Battle

"God made me to be a ski racer," I told my mom when I was eight years old. I vowed I'd race in the Olympics. By the time I was sixteen, I was well on my way to accomplishing that dream. But then tragedy struck. One Saturday morning, I flew off course in a downhill training run and slammed into a tree at fifty miles an hour. The accident crushed my spine and left me paralyzed and dependent on a wheelchair for mobility.

I wanted to die. What kind of future, what kind of quality of life, was I to have? Mostly, I was devastated because my dream was ruined.

Fortunately, my friends and family rallied behind me. After some time to heal emotionally and physically, I was back out there attacking life. And I discovered that if I still wanted to chase my goal, I could compete in the Paralympics, the Olympics for people with physical disabilities.

After much training and many falls, I learned a type of adaptive skiing for individuals with no or limited use of their trunk or lower extremities. I qualified for the U.S. Disabled Ski Team and, in 1998, reached my goal by competing in the Paralympics in Nagano, Japan.

We can choose to let obstacles stop us, or we can find other ways to accomplish our goals. With a supportive team, our only limits are those we place on ourselves.

— MUFFY DAVIS, SKIER

Speaking of Success

As the girls filed in to the auditorium for the Take Our Daughters to Work Day program, I sat in the front row, slugging down Coke in an attempt to wake up and actually make some sense at 9 A.M. A girl sat next to me. I asked her if she was excited to be spending the day at the company.

"Heck, yes," she said. Then she whispered, "So where do you think the lady is?"

"What lady?" I asked, knowing what was coming next.

"You know, the editor of *GL*. She's supposed to be here."

Er, yeah, present and accounted for. "Um, that's me."

The look that came over her face registered somewhere between confusion and horror. She looked at my jeans, T-shirt, ponytail, and lack of lipstick. She blurted, "I thought you were here with your mom."

When I started *Girls' Life*, I was twenty-three. And I looked about sixteen. Trying to persuade people to give you millions of dollars to start a business that 90 percent of people fail at is hard enough. Try doing it when you look like you should be interviewing to be their baby-sitter. Lucky for me, most of my first encounters with people were over the phone. I could use my secret weapon — my deep voice, which made me sound like a seasoned professional. It was usually months before potential investors met me and discovered I was young enough to be their daughter. But by then, I'd proved myself, and we'd laugh over the fact that they'd expected a middle-aged woman.

This year marked the magazine's ninth anniversary. To say we've beaten the odds against success is an understatement. Almost all the other mags that debuted with us have either folded or been sold, but *GL* is a bigger success every year.

— KAREN BOKRAM, MAGAZINE EDITOR

Proud Poem

Just like moons and like suns,
With the certainty of tides,
Just like hopes springing high,
Still I'll rise.

— Maya Angelou, poet, writer, from "Still I Rise"

Female Feat

Cindy Tsai's chess competitors may not take this seventeen-year-old girl seriously at first, but they soon discover they can't judge a chess player by her age or gender. In the male-dominated world of chess, many boys don't believe girls have the smarts to excel at the game. Cindy enjoys beating all kinds of guys, not to mention tons of women. She holds the title of Women's International Master. "I love it when I see girls getting involved in chess," she told *Seventeen*. "Some people say chess is an art; others, that it's a sport or a science. I believe it's all three."

Chapter 15

Handling Competition

 According to Rachel Simmons, author of *Odd Girl Out: The Hidden Culture of Aggression in Girls*, girls strongly value their friendships and the traits friends express, such as being supportive, respectful, and sensitive. But these traits are the opposite of those typically needed for competing with others (and for some aspects of leadership), such as being aggressive, driven, and bold. This creates a conflict for girls because it implies that they can't be both well-liked *and* successful.

You need to be able to strive for success without getting bogged down in excessive competitiveness. But it's also important to feel that you can undertake healthy competition while maintaining relationships. Simmons says, "Giving girls a chance at success means giving them full, equal access to the tools of the game: to the acts of competition and desire required to excel and to the knowledge that relationships can survive them." Instead of trying to brush competitive feelings under the rug to preserve friendships, be direct and honest; don't hide your competitive spirit.

Winning Wisdom

Whatever you want in life, other people are going to want it too. Believe in yourself enough to accept the idea that you have an equal right to it.

— DIANE SAWYER, JOURNALIST

You can stand tall without standing on someone. You can be a victor without having victims.

— HARRIET WOODS, POLITICAL ACTIVIST, WRITER

I don't have to be enemies with someone to be competitors with them.

— JACKIE JOYNER-KERSEE, TRACK-AND-FIELD ATHLETE

If you're too busy worrying about the competition, you don't focus enough on what you're doing. . . . I've always tried to do a really good job every day.

— KATIE COURIC, JOURNALIST, MORNING-SHOW HOST

I know that I will come across athletes who are greater or lesser than I am. If they are lesser, I will be kind and empathetic, and if they are greater, I'm determined to learn from their successes.

— JULIE KRONE, JOCKEY

I'm very aggressive on the track. But I'm friends with a lot of my competitors, and if I'm not friends with them, it just means I don't know them yet.

— SUZY HAMILTON, RUNNER

My favorite rivals are boys because they always think that they are better, stronger, and more fit than girls; I love proving them wrong.

— JENNIFER LAYTON, 12

I've always believed that one woman's success can only help another woman's success.

— GLORIA VANDERBILT, FASHION DESIGNER

Ambition, if it feeds at all, does so on the ambition of others.

— SUSAN SONTAG, WRITER, FILMMAKER

In a close race, I go for everything. . . . When it's that close, it's the most fun.

— JENNIFER SNYDER, DIRT-TRACK RACER

Success Story
Double Victory

Breathe . . . focus . . . count your steps . . . hit the board, and explode! *But not too far.* Not too far? *What am I thinking,* not too far?

These were my thoughts during my eighth-grade league championship track meet. The meet that meant everything at that moment. The meet that could send me to districts and give me a chance to fly to California for the national competition. Only one girl could possibly beat me, and her name was Sharon. I knew Sharon from competing against her in both basketball and track. Next year, we would become teammates at the same high school. She was definitely someone I wanted to be friends with, but would she want to be friends if I prevented her from going on to districts?

I was torn as I prepared to jump. Did I let Sharon win so there would be no hard feelings, or did I jump as well as I could because I wanted to win? As I stood on the runway before my final jump, it all became clear. I needed to do my absolute best. I had trained all season for this moment, and no friendship could interfere with that.

I closed my eyes, took a deep breath, sprinted down the runway, and landed the longest jump of the day. I had beaten Sharon by a quarter of an inch to finish in first place.

As Sharon and I received our medals, she looked disappointed and upset with herself. But she not only congratulated me, she told me how much she was looking forward to our being on the same team next year.

And ultimately, we both won because we had done our best. As it turned out, Sharon's jump was good enough to qualify her for districts even without finishing first. She and I went on to districts together, and we've been best friends ever since.

— ALLISON LUCEY, SPORTS ORGANIZATION CONSULTANT

Female Feat

When Christine Todd Whitman decided that she wanted to be governor of New Jersey, she had very little experience and was considered a long shot to win. However, she surprised her critics and defeated the incumbent, James Florio. Then, when she took over as the state's first female governor, her goal was to reduce taxes by 30 percent within three years; she did it in only two. *People* magazine named Whitman one of its Twenty-five Most Intriguing People, and in 2001, she was appointed administrator of the Environmental Protection Agency (EPA).

FABULOUS FACTS

Psychologist and researcher Sylvia Rimm found that when successful women were growing up, they had commonly been in competitive situations and benefited from knowing what it's like to win.

According to a University of Houston study, 60 percent of those driven to succeed are hypercompetitive: they try to win no matter the circumstances or stakes. The other 40 percent aim to achieve but focus on self-improvement with an eye to future success.

Chapter 16

Coming Up Short

 People think of failure as a big bad no-no. Nobody wants to feel incompetent or mediocre, or look like a loser. But as with everything else, failure has its good side. "Whether it's on a test or not getting the job you want, I think [failure] builds your character," says actor Reese Witherspoon. It can also build your resolve. When you fail, you get back up again, and this time nothing's going to stop you.

Suffragist Susan B. Anthony (1820–1906) put it this way: "Failure is impossible." In other words, if a setback doesn't stop you in your tracks but redirects you or helps you find a new path, it's actually a form of success. You fail only when you don't go after your goals, don't give it your best, or don't bother trying. If you're doing these things, there's no way you can fail, even if you crash and burn miserably — something plenty of people do on their way to success.

Winning Wisdom

Think like a queen. A queen is not afraid to fail. Failure is another stepping-stone to greatness.

— OPRAH WINFREY, TALK-SHOW HOST

If I'm not on the edge of failure, I'm not being sufficiently challenged.

— JEWEL, SINGER-SONGWRITER

It is nothing to succeed if one has not taken great trouble, and it is nothing to fail if one has done the best one could.

— NADIA-JULIETTE BOULANGER, COMPOSER, CONDUCTOR, TEACHER, 1887–1979

Falling's part of the game. It's like my dad always says: "No matter how good you are, the ice is still slippery." The important thing is, it's *your* ice.

— MICHELLE KWAN, FIGURE SKATER

Being defeated is often a temporary condition. Giving up is what makes it permanent.

— MARILYN VOS SAVANT, WRITER

Everything is fixable. Nothing in life is ever set in stone.

— CHRISTINA RICCI, ACTOR

Sometimes it's better to rise up out of the ashes, singing.

— JANE YOLEN, WRITER

Success is often achieved by those who don't know that failure is inevitable.

— COCO CHANEL, FASHION DESIGNER, 1883–1971

Success Stories
Fail It Forward

I remember my preteen and teenage years very well: they were among the most turbulent times in my life. I worked hard to be successful in what I did in school, in my social life, and at home. And when something didn't work, I was pretty frustrated and upset. But over time, I came to see that experiencing failure is an important step in reaching success.

In some ways, achieving success is like finding your way out of a maze. You're going to make wrong turns and run into dead ends. They're the unavoidable price for moving forward. So when you experience a setback, don't pretend it didn't happen. See it with an objective eye and don't make excuses. Look yourself in the mirror and say, "Well, I gave that a good try, but it didn't work. This happens to everybody. Welcome to the human race."

I believe in this approach so much that at my company, Autodesk, I've set up a way of working called "Fail Fast-Forward." The idea is that you try something, and if it doesn't work, you stop doing it right away, understand why it failed, and try something else. We've experienced solid success in our business, and I can truthfully say that one of the reasons is our commitment to Fail Fast-Forward.

When you experience a failure, pick yourself up and get back in the game. With a positive attitude, failures are just temporary wrong turns in the maze leading to success. The secret is not to go out of your way to avoid setbacks; it's to shrug them off and keep moving.

— Carol Bartz, CEO

Stumbling Toward Success

This is neither an acceptance nor a rejection.

I stared in disbelief at the e-mail from the editor of the on-line magazine. How's that for leaving you hanging? I hadn't a clue how to respond. Should I give up? Rewrite the story?

My head told me this was a polite dismissal, but my heart told me to contact her again — even if I risked embarrassment. My mother once said, "People who venture nothing never have to worry but seldom soar. You have to stumble to succeed."

Remaining silent would allow me dignity and safety, but it would also keep me from learning what my mother meant.

My hands trembled as I typed my reply: "If this is neither an acceptance nor a rejection, what is it?"

The editor and I began an e-mail correspondence. While she never published my story (because the publication went out of business), she taught me many wonderful lessons about writing and life, and we became good friends. Most of all, she taught me to get through discouragement and to realize that whether I'm accepted or rejected, my work has merit.

Her words remain etched in my memory: *This is neither an acceptance nor a rejection.*

Success is open-ended like that. If you follow your heart, you'll succeed even if you stumble.

— MICHELE H. LACINA, WRITER

Field and Stream

It was the beginning of my favorite part of the year: softball season. I loved playing softball, standing out there on the field chewing my Dubble Bubble, the afternoon sun beaming down on my head, the smell of freshly cut grass. During tryouts, I was hoping I might get picked to be the captain of the team.

After tryouts, the coaches called each girl into a trailer to tell her if she'd made it. I had no doubt I'd make it because I'd made it last year and I considered myself pretty good. But when I sat down with the coaches, they said, "Sorry, Jessica, you didn't make the team this year."

I was in total shock. I must have asked them "Are you serious?" about fifty times.

When I got home, I was devastated. Softball had been a big part of my life, and now it was just a memory. My mom tried to cheer me up by telling me that "when one door closes, a better one opens," but that didn't make me feel any better. I had missed my chance to try out for other school sports, and I felt like no new doors were going to open.

But, a week later, one *did* open. I heard an announcement on the intercom at school: "Wanna row? If you love crew or just want to try it out, join the Rowers Club." I decided that this was my sign. Now that I had no softball practice, I could do rowing.

I loved it. I loved it even more than softball. It gave me a great group of friends. It took my mind off of everyday stresses. Just being out on the water was a spiritual experience.

I finally found my sport soul mate. Now I know I was cut from softball for a reason: so I could be there when the other door opened.

— Jessica Schnittka, 16

Female Feat

When Sarah Michelle Gellar auditioned for the TV series *Buffy the Vampire Slayer*, she was asked to consider the more superficial character, Cordelia. But she'd already played that type of role and wanted a challenge. At the risk of losing the Cordelia part, she begged to try for the part of Buffy. After "about eleven auditions" she finally got it. "It's always easy to take the route that you know," she says. "But it's also boring! You'll never know what you're capable of if you don't try. So don't be afraid of failure."

Chapter 17

A Winning Image

 In the United States, a girl is generally considered "successful" if she's beautiful, like the girls in ads and movies. This link between physical appearance and perceived worth makes millions of girls obsess about how they look at the expense of what's much more important: knowing who they are and what they want to achieve.

Of course, it makes sense to be attractively groomed and look your best, but don't fall into the trap of evaluating your worth as it measures up to media images. Instead of trying to achieve impossible beauty to feel like a success, reverse the order. Be successful, and then you'll feel radiantly beautiful. Added bonus: you'll also *look* beautiful. When you're vibrantly alive and are enjoying conquering life's challenges, you can't help but turn heads.

Winning Wisdom

They say getting thin is the best revenge. Success is much better.
— OPRAH WINFREY, TALK-SHOW HOST

Character contributes to beauty. . . . A mode of conduct, a standard of courage, discipline, fortitude, and integrity can do a great deal to make a woman beautiful.
— JACQUELINE BISSET, ACTOR

If all you have to offer is a look that is supposed to be appealing, then you are going to be paid attention to [for] about a tenth as long as you would be if when you speak you are interesting.
— JULIA ROBERTS, ACTOR

Look your best, and then you have to suspend your thoughts from it. There's a lot more to think about than your looks.
— ALEXIS BLEDEL, ACTOR

Beauty is the result of realizing what is special about you.
— BOBBI BROWN, ENTREPRENEUR, MAKEUP ARTIST

Nature gives you the face you have when you are twenty. Life shapes the face you have at thirty. But it is up to you to earn the face you have at fifty.

— COCO CHANEL, FASHION DESIGNER, 1883–1971

If I can believe in who I am, what I need, what I deserve, and what I must express, then I can let go of the struggle of self-acceptance based on "their" approval of my beauty. . . . I will dare to do just what I do.

— SABRINA WARD HARRISON, WRITER, ARTIST

I don't believe makeup and the right hairstyle alone can make a woman beautiful. The most radiant woman in the room is the one most full of life and experience.

— SHARON STONE, ACTOR

Moi is not a skinny, skinny girl. Moi is what moi am — full-figured. And moi's frog thinks that is *gangbusters!*

— MISS PIGGY, MUPPET

Beauty can't amuse you, but brainwork — reading, writing, thinking — can.

— HELEN GURLEY BROWN, EDITOR, PUBLISHER

When I lay my head on the pillow at night, I can say I was a decent person today. That's when I feel beautiful.

— DREW BARRYMORE, ACTOR

Success Story
The Shape of Success

When I was in elementary school, I was horribly pigeon-toed. Doctors wanted to put expensive braces on my legs, but my parents didn't have the money. More important, my mother wanted me to depend on myself — not braces — to overcome this problem. She encouraged me to play outside, but I complained. I had endured years of teasing about my feet, and I was embarrassed by my lack of physical skill. So I spent afternoons in front of the television, snacking and gaining weight.

When I was in middle school, my parents suggested I try out for a recreational swim team, and since being pigeon-toed didn't show or matter in the water, I gave it a shot.

That was the turning point.

Daily practice started to slim me down. I went from winning fifth- and sixth-place ribbons to winning seconds and thirds. Suddenly I felt strong and confident, and proud to be part of a team. Then a friend from the swim team suggested I try out for cheerleading. I was initially horrified at the thought because I worried about my coordination, but I decided it would be fun to try.

Surprise: I made the squad (and stayed with it throughout high school). The jumps and routines improved my coordination. My legs grew stronger, and I was able to keep my feet from turning in. And I gained confidence by being in front of crowds.

Swimming and cheerleading completely changed the way I saw myself and how others saw me. Since then, fitness has been a big part of my life. This year, I ran my first triathlon. It gave me the same rush I felt in school, when one small step in the right direction set me in motion on my way to a successful life.

— CRISTINA MENDONSA, TELEVISION NEWS ANCHOR

Female Feat

Clothing designers used to act as if all women were a size ten or smaller, making it tough for the full-figured to find decent outfits. However, in reality, *62 million* American women are a size twelve or larger. And one of them was peeved enough about the discrepancy to take action. "We live in a society that is based upon the attainment of unrealistic beauty," says plus-size supermodel Emme. "I want women to know their self-esteem is not contingent upon their dress size." This television-show host, author, lecturer, and mother has taken matters into her own hands, designing a clothing line exclusively for women sizes twelve to twenty-four. She even has her own Emme doll. Barbie, look out!

FABULOUS FACT

July 3 is national Compliment Your Mirror Day, time to look in the mirror and state something positive about yourself. Feel silly? Who *doesn't* feel like a dork talking to a piece of glass? But the results of this little exercise will reflect brightly on you. Yes, studies actually show it boosts self-esteem. So be like Cameron Diaz, who offers this pointer: "When I look in the mirror for myself, I look at the things I like about myself and try to make them even more fun and even more likable."

Chapter 18

The Social Scene

At your school, it's a safe bet that success is spelled P-O-P-U-L-A-R.

Whether you're enjoying the perks of social success, wishing you fit in with the "in" crowd, or coping just fine with being ignored by the whole scene, a little perspective is in order. There's no evidence that being popular at school has anything to do with whether you're successful in your twenties and beyond.

In fact, believe it or not, if you're uncool, it could give you a jump on success. According to Kris Gowen, Ph.D., the producer of Teensforum.com, "Your problems don't go away just because you're popular. The kids who have to struggle . . . become the most successful as adults."

Don't believe it? Just ask Madonna, Keri Russell, or Alicia Silverstone, none of whom were popular.

Winning Wisdom

When you can hold your head high with confidence that comes from deep inside, not [from] the makeup on your face, then people will flock to you. And remain with you.

— NIKI HORTON, 15

I am living proof that it is possible to profit from being a high school freak.

— MEG CABOT, AUTHOR

Class is an aura of confidence that is being sure without being cocky. Class has nothing to do with money. . . . It's the surefooted-ness that comes with having proved you can meet life.

— ANN LANDERS, ADVICE COLUMNIST, 1918–2002

Beware of over-great pleasure in being popular or even beloved.

— MARGARET FULLER, FOREIGN CORRESPONDENT, EDITOR, 1810–1850

[I'm annoyed] with the importance everyone places on fashion. I almost turn my nose up at all that superficial stuff, to the point where it's like, let me put on my sweatpants and a rag, and pull my hair back and just be real.

— CHRISTINA AGUILERA, SINGER

Worry less about what other people think about you and more about what you think about them.

— FAY WELDON, NOVELIST

Success Stories
Not Just an Act

I stood outside the recreation center with my two friends Natalie and Isabella. We were about to try out for *The Sound of Music,* which was being produced by a local community group. We'd been looking forward to this night for months. *The Sound of Music* had been our favorite movie ever since we met, so the opportunity to act in it was heaven for all of us.

The night flew by in a happy whirl of singing, acting, and hugging my friends. I congratulated Isabella and Natalie, and left with a feeling of hope and confidence.

Neither Natalie nor I was called back to audition for a main part; we'd been cast as chorus members. But Isabella had callbacks for the thirteen-year-old character, Louisa. No doubt, I was disappointed. But instead of focusing on my own slight sadness or feeling jealous or resentful, I devoted all my energy to wishing her well.

One morning a few days later, she ran up to me, red-faced and breathless. "I got the part of Louisa!" she shouted ecstatically.

"Oh my God, good job!" I squealed. "I am so happy for you!"

I meant it, too. In focusing on Isabella instead of myself, I not only got over my disappointment but also felt great about her success. I was floating on a bubble all day. I skipped to my classes and loudly announced the news to anyone who would listen. I think I was happier for her than if I'd gotten the part myself!

— HANA KADOYAMA, 13

The Perfect Prom

All the eighth-grade girls were excited about the prom except me. I knew my parents couldn't afford a gown, and even if they could, who would want to take a fat girl like me to the prom?

"If you want to go, I'll find someone to take you," my mother promised. I knew she meant one of my male cousins. I wanted a boyfriend, even if just for the prom.

My mother was determined to find me a gown, even if it had to come from a discount store. We looked through stacks of dresses. Most were low-cut and more suitable for a glamour girl than for a kid of thirteen, not to mention way more expensive than Mom could afford. We were discouraged until a salesperson showed us a simple gown with a high scooped neckline and skirt of satin and tulle. I held my breath as Mom looked at the price tag. "I'll do the ironing free for a month," I said.

Mom bought it. My entire outfit cost about $25. Best of all, the gown was slimming and made me feel like a princess. So what if I'd have to go with a cousin?

At one of our school assemblies, I met Michael, a nerd who enjoyed reading and was a bit overweight. By the time May came around, we'd become good friends, and he asked me to be his prom date. So much for going with a cousin.

He gave me a pink carnation-and-rose corsage that I wore on my wrist. We danced every dance. We voted for each other for prom king and queen. I hadn't even expected to go to the prom, and instead I had a date, a dress, and a wonderful time.

— Bea Sheftel, teacher

The Outsider

When I was ten, I started middle school. My former classmates and I were thrown into an enormous mixing bowl of kids from four different elementary schools. The social scene was terrifying. There were lots of rich kids. There were girls who already wore makeup and got expensive haircuts, girls whose moms didn't cut their hair out on the porch in the summer like mine did.

The first thing I realized was that I was *different*. The second thing I understood was that *different is bad*. I quickly realized I was not nearly rich or cool enough to be popular. I was embarrassed by my clothes, which I had never cared about before, and I was ashamed that my family didn't live in a nice suburban development. I spent most nights crying because I felt alone and different.

That summer, my mom sent me to camp. I went backpacking and discovered I was an excellent canoeist. I learned that it feels good to climb a mountain. I learned that in the woods, it doesn't matter what brand of clothes you're wearing because everything gets dirty and nobody cares. I learned that difference is good.

After camp, I went home and hated school even more. I found myself doubting that camp had been real. But slowly, gradually, I became sure of myself. It *had* been real. There is another world beyond schools full of kids clamoring to be the most popular and the least different. There is a world where nobody cares about that stuff. There is a world, and I intend to make it mine.

— ERICA FLETCHER, GIRLS' ORGANIZATION PROGRAM DEVELOPER

Chapter 19

Be a Sport

Have you ever noticed the language successful people use?

> *It's not whether you win or lose, but how you play the game.*
> *We scored.*
> *They were good sports.*

Sporty phrases are everywhere because athletics provide a natural training ground for achievers. In individual competitive sports, you learn to push your limits, win triumphantly and lose gracefully, and go after new personal bests. In team sports, you learn additional life skills, such as how to work with others. And even in noncompetitive sports, you learn such success-related things as how good exercise makes you feel about yourself and how practice makes perfect.

So if you want to build success skills — not to mention a bigger vocabulary — play ball (or hockey, or soccer, or whatever)!

Winning Wisdom

Leadership requires working together, facing challenges, and [putting forth] intense effort — many of the same skills required by competitive athletics.

— ROSA DELAURO, CONGRESSWOMAN

People who play team sports know lessons are learned from both winning and losing.

— JOAN DEMPSEY KLEIN, APPEALS COURT JUSTICE

Meeting new people, confidence, self-esteem, time management, discipline, motivation — all these things I learned, whether I knew I was learning [them] or not, through sports.

— MIA HAMM, SOCCER PLAYER

Athletes don't go through that whole thing about worrying how they look; they just want to be strong, and self-confidence is the result.

— KAREN LUNDGREN, ADVENTURE RACER

Everything doesn't always go your way, but I think playing sports helps you to deal with it a lot more easily.

— LISA LESLIE, BASKETBALL PLAYER

Success Stories
The Zen of Fencing

Whenever life became too stressful because of excessive school-work or because things just weren't going my way, I would go over to the fencing club to scare away my frustration in a battle of swords. Over time, I came to really care about this sport. My lessons were the highlight of my week. And so, when I got invited to a novice competition at a university, I was eager to put to use all that I had learned. It was intimidating to be the only high school girl, especially since I was only a freshman. As with any competition, I had no idea what sort of impact I could make or how I would do, until I went out on the strip and did my very best. Each person I fenced was a new, unpredictable challenge. And I enjoyed every moment, proving to myself just what I could do.

At the end of the day, a large engraved trophy with "First Place" on it became mine to take home.

This important aspect of my life was not just participation in a sport. It showed me that if you care about something — not because your grade will be affected by it but because of your own personal interest — being able to face the challenges that come with it only adds to the enjoyment.

— Sara LaHue, 15

Just You Weight . . .

I must admit that it wasn't an easy road to becoming a national champion powerlifter. Many people doubted me, and some told me flat out that I wouldn't be able to accomplish what I was trying to do. I was told it would be difficult to make the top twenty in powerlifting without the use of performance-enhancing drugs. Despite all of this negative feedback, I returned to the gym day after day, four or five days a week. I was determined, and I believed that with focus, I was capable of accomplishing anything I wanted.

In part, I was fueled by my belief that I had to succeed without drugs, even if it took longer. Many people try to achieve success the wrong way, by cheating, stepping on toes, or being deceptive.

This does not work for me. I am first true to myself; then I can be true to others. When you do something right, the hard work pays off and is far more beneficial and long lasting. In my case, I not only made it into the top twenty but stayed there for nine years.

— KATHY ROBERTS, POWERLIFTER

Female Feat

Soccer player Brandi Chastain's big moment came when she made history with a penalty kick that won the 1999 U.S. Women's World Cup. In her jubilation, she pulled off her jersey (as many male soccer players do in this situation). Some people thought she shouldn't have taken her shirt off, while others noted that a sports bra is a common article of apparel and provides more coverage than a bathing suit. The "scandal" only made Brandi more famous. Thanks to her and the rest of the team, women's soccer is now the fastest-growing sport in the United States.

FABULOUS FACTS

Sports can make you feel better about your body image, self-esteem, competency, and success, according to the President's Council on Physical Fitness and Sports. Playing sports can also affect how you do in school: The American Sociological Association found that high school girls' participation in sports was strongly associated with success in science during their sophomore and senior years.

Title IX, the Educational Amendments Act, a landmark law passed in 1972, mandated that girls' sports programs receive funding equal to the amounts designated for boys' programs. Since it went into effect, the number of girls participating in high school sports has shot up from about 300,000 to nearly 2.5 million.

Chapter 20

Join the Team

Personal achievement is cool. But what happens when two or more girls get together on a joint success quest?

Teams can do more and go further than individuals simply because they have more resources: each team member's strengths. The impact is naturally bigger (think peace rallies — one person holding a sign doesn't begin to compare to the image of a chanting mass). Plus, you can have a blast because working together generates energy and cements friendships. Just ask girls who share the same interests, such as scrapbooking or being on the yearbook committee; participate on the same sports teams; or spend hours playing group games like Pictionary and charades.

Isn't it time you joined a team?

Winning Wisdom

Alone we can do so little; together we can do so much.

— HELEN KELLER, WRITER, LECTURER, 1880–1968

No matter what accomplishments you achieve, somebody helps you.

— ALTHEA GIBSON, PROFESSIONAL TENNIS PLAYER AND GOLFER

When I can get out of the water with another two or three people who can work together as a unit on the bike, that's really fun. I love working as a team.

— BARB LINDQUIST, TRIATHLETE

My successes aren't my successes. No one's successes are entirely their own.

— KAREN NUSSBAUM, LABOR ORGANIZATION DIRECTOR

The speed of the leader is the speed of the gang.
— MARY KAY ASH, ENTREPRENEUR, BUSINESS EXECUTIVE, 1915–2001

Effective teamwork is all about making a good, well-balanced salad — not whipping individuals into a single batch of V8.
— SANDRA RICHARDSON, CONSULTANT

Sometimes I lose, but I actually believe what we come out with as a structure is better than what I could have come up with alone.
— RUTH SIMMONS, UNIVERSITY PRESIDENT

Success Story
A Shore Thing

When I was eleven, I was inspired by a newspaper article about a woman who had crossed Lake Ontario in a kayak for the first time. Right then and there, I knew that someday I'd be the one written about after *my* crossing. I hoped girls would read *my* story and be inspired to accomplish their goals.

My team of three was the key in completing this mentally and physically exhausting trip. We looked to one another for support and encouragement, telling jokes and singing songs to boost one another's spirits. The last four hours were the worst. My muscles ached, and every stroke of the paddle hurt. It took mental strength to keep my composure.

But it was all worth it when we reached the Canadian shore. We were the first women's team to kayak across Lake Ontario. I was the youngest person ever to do this. Best of all, the article about me in the paper must have inspired at least a few girls to accomplish *their* goals. And who knows whom *their* articles will inspire?

— EMILY WRIGHT, 14

Female Feat

When American adventurer Ann Bancroft found out that Norwegian adventurer Liv Arnesen was interested in trekking across Antarctica, she suggested they team up and set a goal to be the first women to cross the continent on foot. They skied to the end of the 1,717-mile journey in three months. The secret of their success? "You've got to know your limits and your teammate's limits," says Ann. "It comes down to trust and communication." She also credits her larger team. "All over the world, there were people supporting and following us."

FABULOUS FACT

According to a study by S. Carpenter cited in *The 100 Simple Secrets of Successful People*, those who understand and value the interconnectedness of humanity are twice as likely as people who have the opposite type of belief to feel successful.

Chapter 21

Mind Your Own Business

"Ice-cold lemonade! Fresh-baked cookies!"

If you've ever sold lemonade, or been a baby-sitter, you've taken the first step toward being an entrepreneur — running your own business. You've experienced the thrill of exchanging a product or service for cold, hard cash.

In the United States, the land of opportunity, entrepreneurs are recognized for their success because it's not easy to think up, create, and get funding for a business — and to then turn it profitable and keep it that way. Not all businesses make it, but women clearly have what it takes. Almost 6 percent of American women now own and run their own businesses, accounting for 6.2 million firms. And the Center for Women's Business Research shows that since 1997, female entrepreneurship has grown at double the national average.

If you have dreams of running your own company, you'll be *in* very good company.

Winning Wisdom

Becoming an entrepreneur is the modern-day equivalent of pioneering on the old frontier.

— PAULA NELSON, ECONOMIST

It is not easy to be a pioneer — but oh, it is fascinating! I would not trade one moment, even the worst moment, for all the riches in the world.

— ELIZABETH BLACKWELL, DOCTOR, 1821–1910

I made myself Miss Manners. It was like Napoléon: you crown yourself because nobody else can do it.

— JUDITH MARTIN, COLUMNIST

The trouble with the rat race is that even if you win, you're still a rat.

— LILY TOMLIN, ACTOR

Figure out what your most magnificent qualities are and make them indispensable to the people you want to work with. Notice that I didn't say "work for."

— Linda Bloodworth-Thomason, TV producer

Success Stories
Grand Designs

Ghilotti ink began as a hobby, a joy, and a passion for expression. It was as simple as creating unique invitations, idea journals, and favors for friends during the day, and daring dreams at night. I had essentially told the world and reminded myself that I was capable in character and talent of pursuing my dream of having my own design business.

Now my first real clients were arriving. What was I to do with these people? How was I supposed to run a business? I had never done it before. What if this or that happened?

Very quickly I quit the "what if" game. I charged on and built skills. I got clients — one, two, three, fifteen, and more. I gave each project my all, and I continued to love, love, love what I did.

Clients saw the benefits. Additional clients came knocking. Now I am fueled and fired up to pursue even more: designing my own card line, creating a gift line, and writing books.

When you express your creativity, the biggest reward is the satisfaction of bringing something new into being and of honoring your deepest desires. That is the truest form of success. Being recognized by others is only a side effect.

— MICHELLE GHILOTTI MANDEL, DESIGNER

Out of the Ashes

When I was twenty-six, I lost my job. The computer consulting company where I worked decided they wanted to get out of the consulting business.

I was very sad, then very angry. My team was doing great things for big telecommunications companies. We were establishing a reputation. We did good work at fair prices, and our customers were happy. My husband was sympathetic but didn't know what to say. "I just wish I could keep it going," I explained. "We're in the middle of several big projects. Our customers will be stranded."

Slowly an idea took root in my mind. Maybe, just maybe, I could take over the projects. I could call our customers, offer to finish the projects, try to keep the team together.

The next morning, I went into the office and explained to my consultants that we were being shut down. Their biggest concern was also the unfinished projects. Before I realized what I was saying, I had blurted out my thoughts from the night before. Everyone looked skeptical, and I sent them home.

The next day, my consultants filed into my office one by one. "We could hang around, miss a paycheck," they said. "Work here while we look for something else." When my boss showed up to close the office, I met him with a counterproposal. I didn't know what I was doing, but twenty-four hours later, I'd purchased the contracts and office furniture and taken over the lease agreement.

What began as a desire to just finish what I'd started, quickly turned into a venture employing forty people and bringing in more than $5 million in revenue.

Sometimes having the courage to try something different — to take responsibility and honor your commitment to finish what you start — is all you need to pick the right road in life.

— CARLA CORKERN, SOFTWARE EXECUTIVE

Female Feat

Armed with law and electrical engineering degrees, Lavetta Willis ventured into the male-dominated world of athletic footwear, introducing a shoe line called DaDa. After spending months trying to persuade Sacramento Kings basketball player Chris Webber to endorse the shoes, she finally succeeded. Now the company is one of the hottest footwear and apparel companies in the United States.

FABULOUS FACTS

According to research by Nickelodeon, Yankelovich, and Youth MONITOR, 72 percent of girls ages twelve to seventeen would prefer to start a business instead of work for someone else.

How many girls already own a business? One percent, according to Teenage Research Unlimited.

A survey called "Teen Girls on Business: Are They Being Empowered?" at Simmons School of Management in Boston found that minority girls look to entrepreneuring as a path to success more often than nonminorities do. While 39 percent of Caucasians were interested in starting their own businesses, the figures were higher for blacks (56 percent), Hispanics (50 percent), and Asians (41 percent).

Through 2007, Hispanic female–owned small businesses are expected to grow at a whopping 30 percent, outpacing all other business segments, according to Insight Research Corporation.

Chapter 22

Lead the Followers

The words *leadership* and *power* pretty much scream, "Success!"

The trouble is, they don't conjure up the best or most accurate images. Think of a leader or a powerful person and you probably imagine someone barking orders or on the phone cutting deals with other powerful people. *Power* is associated with appearing busy and influential, says former congresswoman Patricia Schroeder. "When you peel it all away, [powerful-looking people] usually don't know what they're doing." There's a difference between attempting to have power *over* and having the ability to get things done.

True leaders may be either go-getters who aren't afraid to take charge and act the part or quieter souls who downplay their organizational abilities with comments like "I'm just doing the best I can." Either way, what gives them away is their focus on getting results and working productively with others to achieve goals.

Do you recognize yourself here?

Winning Wisdom

Some leaders are born women.

— GERALDINE FERRARO, BUSINESSWOMAN, POLITICAL ANALYST

To be a leader, you must feel that you are both everything and nothing — nothing in that you are on this earth for a few years out of billions . . . everything because you are at the center of all activity in your world.

— EDITH WEINER, BUSINESSWOMAN

You don't have to be able to do everybody else's job very well. What you have to do is put it all together effectively and smartly.

— LOIS JULIBER, BUSINESS EXECUTIVE

In the Information Age, the rules call for leaders who develop teams and partners, rather than those who command decisions and wield absolute authority.

— JENNY MING, COMPANY DIVISION PRESIDENT

A leader is not [always] the captain or the star of the team, a leader is [also] someone who organizes a game, remembers to bring the ball, or does a good job on the team.

— Brandi Chastain, soccer player, coach

Any committee is only as good as the most knowledgeable, determined, and vigorous person on it. There must be somebody who provides the flame.

— Lady Bird Johnson, former first lady

Nobody gives you power. You just take it.

— Roseanne, actor, talk-show host

Success Story
Confessions of a Captain

I arrived at the National Student Leadership Conference late. Exhausted, hungry, and clad in jeans, I walked into a room of twenty people, all dressed in formal business attire.

I was the youngest one there, having finished only my freshman year of high school. Our group was assigned to form a mock company and make a pitch to kids designated as venture capital-ists. That night, I couldn't have guessed how much my team would accomplish in the next four days, or how I would grow as an in-dividual.

Early on, I emerged as the organizer — the one pulling everyone together—the leader. I split our new company into subgroups, each with its own responsibilities. I made sure each team got what it needed; I offered advice and listened to suggestions. I made sure everything was getting done, and done well. I helped people with their parts of the presentation. When it came time to rehearse, everyone was impressed by my public speaking skills. I had leadership qualities and talents that we needed.

Here, the girl with the nicest hair or the cutest laugh wasn't the star, I was: the girl with the analytical capabilities and speaking skills. My teammates predicted I'd become a politician, and after those four days, I believed it could happen.

I told my parents about that week, but I'm not sure if they ever believed I actually led the group. But inside, *I* know what hap-pened, and it gives me strength. I'm a student leader today, and maybe a world leader tomorrow.

— SARAH WETENHALL, 15

Female Feat

An NFL football team like the Oakland Raiders needs a strong leader, and that's exactly what it's got. Her name is Amy Trask — America's only female CEO of a pro football team. As the lone woman in this male-dominated world, she's not only learned how to make herself heard but proved she can negotiate major deals. Amy is so committed to the team that when a game went into overtime right before her wedding, she wouldn't leave the stadium until the Raiders won — a cool half-hour before the ceremony.

FABULOUS FACTS

Has a woman ever been a U.S. president? Unofficially, yes. Edith Wilson (1872–1961), the wife of President Woodrow Wilson, secretly took over for him when he had a stroke in 1919.

Calling all girls! The U.S. government makes major decisions affecting girls' lives, such as what's taught in school and whether there is money for girls' sports programs. However, women are still only a minority of officeholders (14 percent of the Senate and 13.6 percent of the House of Representatives in 2003), so the female perspective is often missing or overruled. "Women make a difference as elected officials because it's one thing to be sympathetic to the problems women encounter and another to have gone through them," says Linda Sanchez, a U.S. congresswoman (and sister of Congresswoman Loretta Sanchez). Aunt Sam needs you!

According to a study at Maastricht University (in the Netherlands) and New York University, successful leaders are people who treat others fairly and give them a chance to participate in decision making. This is good news for girls who want to lead. Why? In groups, girls and women often do these things naturally.

Chapter 23

Bank On It

Right now, you may view money mainly as something that buys clothes and other goodies, but it's also a critical resource for attaining success.

It gives you flexibility (for example, if you want to quit a job but need to keep paying rent while you find another). It can motivate you (there's nothing like having some money in the bank). It can pay the costs of launching a business. Most important, it lets you take care of yourself.

No bones about it, money can have a serious impact on whether or not you ascend your personal staircase of success. A word of caution, however: money won't buy you happiness. This means you'll probably be more content spending your days doing something you love that doesn't make you rich as opposed to doing something you hate that does. The key is to strike a healthy balance between what you're doing and what you're earning.

Get economically empowered today.

Winning Wisdom

We're taught that someone will be there to help us, someone like Prince Charming. But really, our greatest ally is ourselves.

— ANN RICHARDS, POLITICIAN

Women are taught [that] if we look good, we'll be OK. But looking good is no security. A woman will have fewer wrinkles on her face if she has money in her checking account.

— JOAN PERRY, INVESTING EXPERT

Even though money is the root of all evil, it's also a way to survive.

— BRANDY, SINGER, ACTOR, MODEL

To know you can support yourself is vital. Vital!

— BARBARA WALTERS, REPORTER, TALK-SHOW HOST

I can't think of anything that has helped me in my business life more than learning not to be afraid of money and understanding its place and priorities.

— KATHY IRELAND, ENTREPRENEUR, MODEL

To fulfill a dream, to be allowed to sweat over lonely labor, to be given a chance to create, is the meat and potatoes of life. The money is the gravy.

— BETTE DAVIS, ACTOR, 1908–1989

Money comes and goes. I don't care whether I'm picking up trash or on a stage singing, my biggest dream is to be happy with whatever I do.

— KELLY OSBOURNE, SINGER

Think bigger! Be a millionaire, don't marry one.

— NELL MARINO, ORGANIZATION COFOUNDER, CEO

Money itself cannot make you financially free. Only you can make yourself financially free, and you can do it — and so much more.

— SUZE ORMAN, FINANCIAL EXPERT

Success Story
An Investment in the Future

Before I started investing, I thought it was boring and confusing. During the summer I turned thirteen, my parents said they wanted me to start investing so I wouldn't spend my vacation "wasting my time and their money." They set up an account at an on-line brokerage house. Every day, my dad taught me how to track stocks, look for "good" companies, and place orders on-line. Soon I was reading all the magazine and newspaper articles I could find about the stock market.

When I started high school, I saw that many of my peers were extremely wasteful with money. They would go out and spend extravagant amounts of their parents' — or sometimes their own — hard-earned dollars on expensive clothes and electronic equipment. So I decided to start an investment club at school to teach students how important it is to save and invest money so it will grow.

So many club members joined not even knowing what a stock was and turned into promising young investors. One girl joined just because her best friend was the club's treasurer. She became our investing hero and ended up asking her dad to open a real account for her.

Knowing how to invest not only helped me understand the importance of saving and not wasting money but also completely affected the direction of my life. For example, I realized I could save a lot of money by applying for scholarships to help pay for college. Now I have a scholarship, and I put the money I *didn't* have to spend on tuition into savings so it will accrue interest. My major will be business/finance, and one day I'll land my dream job as an investment banker.

— ATHENA YANG, 17

Female Feat

Ever heard the saying "Do what you love, and the money will follow"? Oprah did, and the money did. When she was twelve, she spoke at a church and was paid $500. She promptly told her father she wanted to talk for a living and that she "planned to be very famous." Now one of the richest women on the planet, she says: "I would do what I'm doing even if I weren't getting paid."

FABULOUS FACTS

According to a study by Yankelovich, girls' number one concern is that they won't have enough money at some point in their lives.

According to Girls Inc. and OppenheimerFunds, 75 percent of women wish they'd learned more about money while growing up.

According to the International Mass Retail Association, teen girls (ages thirteen through seventeen) spend about $25 each time they go to the mall, two to three times per week. Over five years, this adds up to about $18,000. If this amount were saved and ac- crued interest of only 5 percent over fifteen years, it would grow to more than $38,000.

In a 2002 poll by Junior Achievement, teen girls were found to earn only 83 cents for every dollar teen boys earn.

Chapter 24

Any Volunteers?

 So far, this book has focused on success as it relates to getting ahead. But there's also another type of success: helping improve life for others.

Sometimes these two things are one and the same, such as if you invent something that not only makes everyday life easier but also makes money. However, the majority of helpful efforts — such as feeding the hungry, assisting battered women, and funding research on kids' health—aren't set up to haul in bucks but simply to assist those in need.

People who succeed in this category get their feelings of satisfaction from seeing the smiles on the faces of those they help and from knowing that they're literally impacting lives, if not just one then many.

Whether you choose a career at a nonprofit or simply volunteer time to help people on weekends, you'll succeed on a whole new level.

Winning Wisdom

Wouldn't it be awesome if we all thought, *When I grow up, I want to be someone's hero?* I'm not saying rush in to dangerous situations without thinking. . . . I'm just saying it really doesn't matter how rich, thin, or famous you are. What matters is that you make your life matter.

— JAMIE-LYNN SIGLER, ACTOR

We must use our lives to make the world a better place, not just to acquire things. That is what we are put on earth for.

— DOLORES HUERTA, UNION ORGANIZER, LOBBYIST

Our own success, to be real, must contribute to the success of others.

— ELEANOR ROOSEVELT, FIRST LADY, HUMANITARIAN, 1884–1962

It's a hollow thing, ambition just for itself alone.

— SELA WARD, ACTOR

All of us want to do well. But if we do not do good, too, then doing well will never be enough.

— ANNA QUINDLEN, WRITER

Career paths don't have to go in straight lines. Getting involved outside your organization makes you more valuable to your organization.

— JAMIE GORELICK, FORMER VICE CHAIR OF THE
FANNIE MAE FOUNDATION

When I die, if I can say that this little sand on the beach was able to make a couple of waves of change, that's fine.

— ANTONIA HERNANDEZ, CIVIL RIGHTS ORGANIZATION PRESIDENT,
LAWYER

Go for it, never back down, and don't give in, because there's no greater satisfaction in life than using your gifts to help others and to contribute to your community and country.

— MADELEINE ALBRIGHT, FORMER SECRETARY OF STATE

Girls are the agents of change. They are our most potent force for making a difference in the world.

— JANE FONDA, ACTOR

Success Stories
Suitcases for Success

When I was nine, I learned that children in protective (foster) care move from home to home carrying their belongings in trash bags. I thought that was horrible. I wanted to provide these kids with some self-respect and dignity, so I decided to get a suitcase for every foster child in my county.

I named my project "Suitcases for Kids," put up posters about it, and spoke at schools, churches, and civic groups. With the help of various organizations, I collected and delivered 175 suitcases to be handed out by social services.

To expand the effort, I addressed a statewide convention of social services directors. I passed out copies of a "starter kit" to guide others in gathering suitcases. Soon I had hundreds more suitcases. The project spread nationwide and into other countries, prompting Oprah Winfrey to name me an Angel and have me on her show.

Now I'm seventeen and the CEO of Suitcases for Kids (www. suitcasesforkids.org), a nonprofit active in all fifty states and in forty-two other countries. My duties include office work, travel, fundraising, and making speeches, as well as distributing bags.

People often ask why Suitcases for Kids is so successful. One reason is that it showcases endless examples of volunteers who've achieved a sense of fulfillment by donating time, energy, and ideas to improve the lives of foster children. Looking back, I realize that Suitcases for Kids proved that one person actually *can* make a difference.

— Aubyn Burnside, 17

Habitat for Happiness

After six years of elementary school, two years of junior high, four years of high school, five years of college (yes, five), and three years of law school, I was finally ready for a career. I just didn't have any idea what it would be. I had enjoyed law school, but I didn't want to practice law. But what would I do instead?

I knew I couldn't just sit around baking and knitting, so I continued to do what I always did in my spare time — I volunteered at the local Habitat for Humanity office.

I decided I wanted a career in the nonprofit sector. I tried to get a job with Habitat for Humanity, but they didn't have the funds to pay me. Finally, I landed two part-time fundraising jobs with other organizations. I wasn't qualified "on paper" — I had never done the things I was hired to do — but I knew I had the right skills. I continued to volunteer for Habitat for Humanity. Then, lo and behold, a representative from Habitat's headquarters was in our area looking for a fundraiser. My volunteering experience made me perfect for the job.

My career path was not straight, but I was always headed in the same direction — toward what I enjoyed. If you keep plugging away at something long enough, someone will eventually pay you to do it.

— Nancy Martz, fundraiser

Female Feat

Singer-songwriter Ani DiFranco, who has done volunteer work in support of Central American solidarity and war resistance, believes everyone has a responsibility to address social issues in whatever she or he does. Her way of giving back is to not only be a punk rocker but to talk about issues that are vitally important to her, bringing them to the attention of large numbers of people. She facilitates audience interaction at her shows. "I prefer the power that comes from walking onstage . . . and really trying to communicate with people. For me, that's more punk rock than just making a lot of noise."

FABULOUS FACTS

Young people who volunteer are more likely to do well in school, graduate, vote, and be philanthropic says a study by UCLA and the Higher Education Research Institute. In addition, notes the *Journal of Research on Adolescence,* volunteers have a healthier work ethic and more perseverance with long-term goals.

In a Roper National Youth Opinion Survey, approximately a third of kids in grades seven through twelve said that "working for the good of my community and country" and "helping others or volunteering" were key goals for them.

Chapter 25

Winner's Circle

So you won a chess tournament, scored an A+ on a history test, received the Most Valuable Player award, or landed the lead role in the school production? Your team beat its longtime rival, or you got a standing ovation? Congratulations. You're a winner!

Winning is a blast. It sends your self-confidence soaring and makes you feel like you're floating. And, in essence, you are . . . because at that point you've zoomed past the moon and have headed out into the stars.

WHAT? You only placed third in the tournament, got a B– on the test, barely passed physical education, or got the part of a dwarf with only two lines in the school play? Horrors. Technically this could be called losing, but it's *not* the end of the world. You may be disappointed, but please don't give up. You'll have lots more opportunities to win.

This chapter is dedicated to all the times you've been and will be a winner, and to all the time you've spent waiting patiently, only to emerge victorious.

Winning Wisdom

Yesterday I dared to struggle. Today I dare to win.
— BERNADETTE DEVLIN, POLITICIAN

Progress is not always a straight line in which we must defeat or outstrip others and there is only one winner. Progress is a circle in which we strive to use all our talents and complete ourselves. Potentially, we are all winners.
— GLORIA STEINEM, WOMEN'S RIGHTS ACTIVIST, WRITER

Winning is great, but if you are really going to do something in life, the secret is learning how to lose.
— WILMA RUDOLPH, SPRINTER, BASKETBALL PLAYER, 1940–1994

The first thing I do after losing . . . is to forget it. I take a look at my calendar and start thinking about where we'll be playing next week, and I'll show 'em then!
— NANCY LOPEZ, GOLFER

Winning is neither everything nor the only thing. It is one of many things.

— JOAN BENOIT SAMUELSON, RUNNER

If you don't quit, and don't cheat, and don't run home when trouble arrives, you can only win.

— SHELLEY LONG, ACTOR

Winning may not be everything, but losing has little to recommend it.

— DIANNE FEINSTEIN, SENATOR

I cherish the bronze medal as much as the gold medal.

— TERESA WEATHERSPOON, BASKETBALL PLAYER

Most of us are born without greatness, and if we can learn to be second best (or third, or even undistinguished) with grace — that is, with the same dedication, hard work, and discipline we would apply to being first — then the result would make a very fine civilization indeed.

— DIANE WAKOSKI, POET

There's no greater thing than having a whole arena on their feet, screaming!

— SARAH HUGHES, FIGURE SKATER

Success Stories
The Sound of Silence

In seventh grade I really wanted to be in the school play, *42nd Street*. I auditioned with ten students I didn't know. I sing very low, so I was worried about the high notes of my song, "A Whole New World," but I had practiced and was ready.

I was the last person to sing. I was doing tremendously, but then I stumbled on one of the high notes and all that came out was air. I turned red and stopped, but the producers told me to keep going. When I got to another killer note, I heard air again.

When I finished singing, I exploded in tears. All I thought about was what a horrible job I'd done. The other people auditioning comforted me, but I couldn't stop crying; I thought I had blown my chance.

Five days later, I was surprised to get a call from the producers, asking me to come back and try out for a lead part. I thought I was dreaming. Had they really called? Yes! I had to sing a song and recite some lines. Two days later, they gave me the part.

Amid all my excitement, I realized that mistakes and imperfections are not the end of the world. Without them, I would not have learned so much, and my success might not have seemed as sweet.

— KELSEA ERIN EDGERLY, 13

Tooting My Own Horn

As though arriving at a huge middle school weren't enough, I was the only girl in the trumpet section, with too-curly red hair and legs my mother wouldn't let me shave. A trillion years had zoomed past since I was eight, when my favorite uncle had put his trumpet in my hands and encouraged me to push the valves and blow. I looked at the bell of my tuba and wished I could crawl in.

"Next," the director said, looking at me. The room was *way* too quiet as I played the designated selections. I concentrated and got through it, not missing notes but thinking that if I had supported better from my diaphragm, the tone would have been much better.

The results were posted in the band room at the end of the school day: trumpet section, chairs one through nine. My name was next to number one. Oh, that felt great! The practice had paid off. Who knows how I might've done without curly red hair or worries about leg hair sticking out?

— JAN WALKER, BUSINESS OWNER

Female Feat

The winningest female athlete of the first half of the twentieth century was Mildred "Babe" Didrikson Zaharias (1911–1956), who excelled not in one sport but in scads of them: track and field, basketball, tennis, baseball, softball, diving, roller-skating, and bowling, not to mention golf, which she learned how to play in her "retirement" after becoming world famous in track and basketball. Her secret? "The formula for winning is simple: practice and concentration, then more practice and concentration."

Chapter 26

Now What?

 It's been a few days now, and you're starting to come off of the highs you felt when you achieved your goal. Maybe you're getting restless and a little bored.

That's OK because success is best as a *lifestyle*, not just a one-time thing. A truly successful person never rests on her laurels but instead piles successes on top of each other. As mountain climber Arlene Blum puts it, "You never conquer a mountain. You stand on the summit a few moments; then the wind blows your footprints away."

The wind has come up, and the sun is setting on your day of glory. Get busy making some new tracks toward the peaks in the distance.

Happy trails . . .

Winning Wisdom

I'm always making a comeback, but nobody ever tells me where I've been.

— BILLIE HOLIDAY, BLUES SINGER, 1915–1959

I am not a has-been. I'm a will-be.

— LAUREN BACALL, ACTOR

People who are very able and talented and smart and gifted . . . need to take responsibility for creating new games for themselves.

— JENNA ELFMAN, ACTOR

Success is important only to the extent that it puts one in a position to do more things one likes to do.

— SARAH CALDWELL, OPERA FOUNDER, DIRECTOR, CONDUCTOR

If I'm lucky, as long as I keep finding things to challenge me and tickle my fancy, I'll continue until they put me out to pasture.

— SUSAN SARANDON, ACTOR, ACTIVIST

I am always more interested in what I am about to do than in what I have already done.

— RACHEL CARSON, ENVIRONMENTALIST, MARINE BIOLOGIST, 1907–1964

Success only breeds a new goal. The golden apple devoured has seeds. It is endless.

— BETTE DAVIS, ACTOR, 1908–1989

I am a person who wants to continue to reach. I want to stay in awe. When I'm not in awe anymore, I'll be asking myself if I'm done.

— TERESA WEATHERSPOON, BASKETBALL PLAYER

Our deeds still travel with us from afar / And what we have been makes us what we are.

— GEORGE ELIOT (PEN NAME OF MARY ANN EVANS), WRITER, 1819–1880

There is no point at which you can say, "Well, I'm successful now. I might as well take a nap."

— CARRIE FISHER, ACTOR

Female Feats

Remember your first day of school? Ruby Bridges certainly does. It was 1960 in New Orleans, she was six, and schools in the South that had formerly taught only white children had just been ordered to admit black children. Ruby was the only black girl daring to venture in, along with her mom. They were escorted by federal marshals through groups of people protesting her presence.

She was a hero that day, but that day was only the beginning. All the parents of the white kids took their children out of the school, leaving Ruby as the only student. Her brand of success wasn't a one-day event. She continued going to the school by herself every day for the rest of the school year. Her braveness not only paid off for her own education but also helped educate America about racism and started the wheel of equal rights turning.

Where does a golfer go once she's the best female player in the world? Annika Sörenstam pushed beyond what some would see as complete and total success. She started playing golf when she was twelve and worked her way up to win not only Sweden's most prestigious sports award, "Athlete of the Year," but also scads of international women's tournaments. Next on her agenda? Expand her playing field by taking on a new challenge: *male* pro golfers. So when she was invited to play in the traditionally all-male Bank of America Colonial Golf Tournament in Forth Worth, Texas, in 2003, she accepted, becoming the first woman in fifty-eight years to compete in a men's golf event.

While she didn't rank high enough to move beyond the initial round, she still won like crazy. Her presence caused a huge stir in the golf world and brought new status to both the Ladies Professional Golf Association (LPGA) and women's athletics in general. She won by being cool and classy, ignoring her many male critics, and concentrating on her performance. But most of all, she won by simply choosing to go as far as she could. "I just wanted to push myself and do what I love to do the best," she said. Who knows what other successes await her in the future?

Sometimes when it seems someone's at the height of her career, she goes higher. A good example is Hillary Rodham Clinton. No other first lady has "retired" from the White House, where she was a highly visible and influential first lady, to run for and win a seat in the U.S. Senate (New York). What's next?

Chapter 27

Go!

You've now finished examining all the items in your success toolbox. All the handy helpers are in there.

Now the question is, what kind of successful life do you want to build?

For clues, imagine you're ninety years old, looking back on your achievements, fame, fortune, family — whatever you've created. Notice what it looks and feels like. What have you accomplished? What are you most proud of?

Now pull out your success tools and get to work. Start pouring the foundation from which to launch your life's grand undertakings. Set goals and break them into minigoals. Start putting your plans in motion. Train for a triathlon. Write a poem. Lead a team to victory. Volunteer for a local election campaign. Enter a contest. Give it your all.

Build a future so stunning that when you finally turn around to see where you've been, you're dazzled by the very sight.

The toolbox is open, and the shiny tools are glinting in the sunlight.

Winning Wisdom

Today you lay claim to the future. You take a step — nothing more, nothing less — toward making that future your own. But what a step!

— KATHERINE D. ORTEGA, FORMER U.S. TREASURER, BANK EXECUTIVE

More Resources

Books

TEEN POWER POLITICS: MAKE YOURSELF HEARD, by Sara Jane Boyers (Millbrook Press, 2000).

GIRL POWER: WOMEN ON WINNING, by Carmine DeSena and Jennifer DeSena (Andrews McMeel, 2001).

GIRLWISE: HOW TO BE CONFIDENT, CAPABLE, COOL, AND IN CONTROL, by Julia DeVillers (Prima, 2002).

TEEN SUCCESS! JUMP START IDEAS TO MOVE YOUR MIND, by Beatrice J. Elyé with Catherine A. Southwick (Great Potential Press, 2001).

THROW LIKE A GIRL: DISCOVERING THE BODY, MIND AND SPIRIT OF THE ATHLETE IN YOU, by Shelley Frost and Ann Troussieux (Beyond Words, 2000).

Girl Boss: Running the Show Like the Big Chicks: Entrepreneurial Skills, Stories, and Encouragement for Modern Girls, by Stacy Kravetz (Girl Press, 1999).

Cool Careers for Girls, by Ceel Pasternak et al. (series from Impact Publications).

50 Great Businesses for Teens: How to Start Your Own Business — and Make Big Bucks! by Sarah L. Riehm (Macmillan, 1997).

See Jane Win for Girls: A Smart Girl's Guide to Success, by Dr. Sylvia Rimm (Free Spirit, 2003).

Moneymakers: Good Cents for Girls, by Ingrid Roper (Pleasant Company, 1998).

Organizations

Girls' Pipeline to Power, www.girlspipeline.org. A great site created by the Patriot's Trail Girl Scout Council, Inc.

Independent Means, www.independentmeans.com/ask/index. html. Q&As with successful female entrepreneurs and other info for girls who want to start businesses.

New Moon, www.newmoon.org. An award-winning magazine and Web site loaded with info to help girls succeed.

Take Our Daughters and Sons to Work Day, www.daughtersand sonstowork.org. The official site for this important annual go-to-work event.

VolunteerMatch, www.volunteermatch.org. Type in your zip code to find local volunteer opportunities.

The White House Project, www.thewhitehouseproject.org. An easy-to-navigate site dedicated to girls' leadership.

Your Expedition, www.yourexpedition.com. Inspiring info about Ann and Liv's (see pages 134–135) upcoming projects.

Copyright Acknowledgments

Index

Catherine Dee loves providing girls with inspirational books that she would have enjoyed as a teen. In addition to this book, she's written *The Girls' Guide to Life, The Girls' Book of Wisdom, The Girls' Book of Friendship,* and *The Girls' Book of Love.* Catherine lives in Northern California with her husband, Jonathan.

You can reach Catherine via her Web site, *www.deebest.com;* e-mail address, cate@deebest.com; or regular mail care of Megan Tingley Books, Little, Brown and Company, 1271 Avenue of the Americas, New York, NY 10020.

Don't miss:

The Girls' Book of Love

"Readers will enjoy the sage advice and sigh at the bliss recounted as they are guided through all the stages of love, from the first stirrings of a crush to a breakup, and they will return to these pages when they are looking for inspiration or comfort."

— School Library Journal

"Whether you're madly in love or still looking, you'll dig this collection of stories and quotes."

— Twist

"Valentine wisdom."

— Teen People

The Girls' Book of Friendship

"An inspiring collection."

— Publishers Weekly

"Girls will return to its pages again and again when they are looking for just the right words to say 'thanks,' a bit of inspiration, and practical advice as well."

— School Library Journal

The Girl's Book of Wisdom

An ALA Popular Paperback for Young Adults and a Quick Pick for Reluctant Young Adult Readers

A winner of the *Disney Adventures* Best Book Award

"This collection is upbeat and lighthearted. . . . The handy size combined with the accessible format will appeal to this age group."
— *School Library Journal*

"The Girls' Book of Wisdom features quotes from a dynamic group of intelligent women. Each idea has something positive to offer girls.
— *Ann Richards, former governor of Texas*

The Girls' Guide to Life

A *San Francisco Chronicle Book Review* "Best Bet"

"The Girls' Guide to Life is like having a best girlfriend for every activity you can think of. . . . A friendly, commonsense approach for girls who are learning and exploring the basics of life."
— *Gloria Steinem*

"Fact-packed and thought-provoking . . . a pleasing and valuable guide."
— *Kirkus*